THOMAS WOLFE

MEMOIR OF A FRIENDSHIP

THOMAS WOLFE

MEMOIR OF A FRIENDSHIP

by Robert Raynolds

UNIVERSITY OF TEXAS PRESS

AUSTIN & LONDON

PERMISSIONS

Acknowledgment is made to the following publishers for permission to quote from titles in which copyrights appear as indicated:

Harper & Brothers
  The Hills Beyond, by Thomas Wolfe, copyright 1935, 1936, 1937, 1939, 1941 by Maxwell Perkins, Executor, Estate of Thomas Wolfe.
Charles Scribner's Sons
  Look Homeward, Angel, by Thomas Wolfe, copyright 1929 by Charles Scribner's Sons; renewal copyright © 1957 Edward C. Aswell.
  Of Time and the River, by Thomas Wolfe, copyright 1935 by Charles Scribner's Sons; renewal copyright © 1963 Paul Gitlin.
  The Story of a Novel, by Thomas Wolfe, copyright 1936 by Charles Scribner's Sons; renewal copyright © 1964 Paul Gitlin.
  From Death to Morning, by Thomas Wolfe, copyright 1935 by Charles Scribner's Sons; renewal copyright © 1963 Paul Gitlin.
  The Letters of Thomas Wolfe, edited by Elizabeth Nowell, copyright 1956 by Edward C. Aswell.
I acknowledge with appreciation permission granted by Paul Gitlin, Administrator C.T.A., Estate of Thomas Wolfe, to quote from inscriptions which Thomas Wolfe penned to me in copies of his books and from unpublished letters from Wolfe to me, and to use a photograph of Thomas Wolfe in Asheville.
I am grateful to Thomas Wolfe's friend Belinda Jelliffe for permission to reproduce a rare photograph she took of Thomas Wolfe, and to my friend Althea Clark to reproduce a photograph she took of me.

Robert Raynolds

In Memory of Thomas Wolfe, 1900–1938
and
In Honor of Our Friendship

Thomas Wolfe wanted to be known and remembered with affection.

We were children of mountain places. He was born in the haunting depth of the Great Smoky Mountains of North Carolina, and I was born at the foot of the Sangre de Cristo Mountains where they endorse their majesty on the sky of New Mexico. Mountains were our cradle; and we loved the earth, our home.

We were small-town boys, and learned our lives in the midst of ordinary people.

We both knew the toil and joy of writing novels, and we brought to each other the comfort and laughter of being friends.

We had devoted our lives to saying the word of our manhood for ourselves and other men to live by; in this devotion there was no personal, no literary, nor any worldly competition between us: our friendship was grounded on bottom rock of love, that we helped, and wanted to help, each other live.

In this book I honor our friendship, and I remember Thomas Wolfe, with affection, to the world.

CONTENTS

1. "Watch for the Name of Thomas Wolfe!" 5

2. The Legend and the Man 12

3. Heaving His Troubled Tongue 22

4. The Web of Earth 29

5. The Lost Boy 45

6. A Psychic Disturbance 51

7. Mountain Journey 69

8. The Crisis 101

9. The Mottled Sky 112

10. Repeated Pleasure 121

11. Thomas Wolfe and Maxwell Perkins—
    Men of High Order 133

12. A Good Man: End and Eternal 140

ILLUSTRATIONS

(Following page 70)

Early spring in the Great Smoky Mountains
Thomas Wolfe as a young man
Robert Raynolds as a young man
Thomas Wolfe in North Carolina
Robert Raynolds in New Mexico
Thomas Wolfe after years of writing
Robert Raynolds after years of writing
Early autumn in the Sangre de Cristo Mountains

THOMAS WOLFE

MEMOIR OF A FRIENDSHIP

THE TWO MEN

THOMAS WOLFE, in a copy of his book *From Death to Morning* that he presented to Robert Raynolds, wrote:

Nov. 12, 1935

Dear Bob: — The greatest honor you ever did me was to be my friend—the next greatest was to dedicate to me a book in which you had put some of the beauty, passion and aspiration of your experience. All I can here do or say is to tell you that I am proud and happy to owe you this great debt—and to hope that here in this short book—and in my later ones—you may find increasing justification for your faith, your friendship, and your belief.

Tom

ROBERT RAYNOLDS, in the course of a long passage about Thomas Wolfe in his book *In Praise of Gratitude* (1961), wrote:

Our friendship was a comfort, one to the other, of two strangely tall men, who beat about the places and times of man on earth, smitten with sorrow and adance with wonder, trying to tell it, say it, sing it. . . . When we met, neither one of us was alone, for we met in the deep ranges of intuition and insight, we met in confirmation of one another, in trust and in song . . . Sometimes still in the night I dream his face and dream his voice and dream his goodness in converse beside me; and again, after so many years, wake to the knowing of grief that my friend is dead.

1. "WATCH FOR THE NAME OF THOMAS WOLFE!"

This is a story no one else could tell.

Once upon a time I knew a lonesome man. I saw him often; we laughed together; I liked him well. He wrote of the world we live in and of human life in terms of hunger, fury, guilt, in terms of pride, pain, and death. I think he was a religious poet, who sang of hell. He had also a lovely chortle of delight in the sudden amazement of our earthly life. He died young. His name was Thomas Wolfe.

What did Wolfe look like in his room or on the street, or eating or walking in the morning in a pine forest? What were the sounds of his voice and the tilt of his head and the swing of his arm? What when sorrow dug, or anger, or revenge, or laughter lit up his soul? What was the blaze of life in that man's eye?

I feel sure there are many readers of Thomas Wolfe who would enjoy a narrative which could answer such and kindred questions in passing; and to them I present here my story of how I happened to meet Wolfe, how our friendship grew, was threatened by a crisis, survived that crisis, and continued until his death. I am not going to invent incidents or throw in legends to make the story astonishing. It will take all the art I have to portray the man I remember and tell the grace of life we worked out between us in trust of one another. And I must draw my own portrait, as well as his, for this is the story of two men being friends.

In the winter of 1927 or 1928, before I had heard the name of Thomas Wolfe, I chanced to meet a woman he loved. I have never seen her again, but later, when Wolfe sometimes alluded to her, I would remember how she appeared to me in the one meeting.

It was on a winter night in New York; the towers sparkled and snow was falling down onto the lighted streets. Many people with eager faces were walking in the Broadway glimmer, among snowflakes, toward entertainment. There were big snowflakes which stayed long enough on my overcoat sleeve to be seen clearly before they melted; and when I glanced down at Marguerite, my wife, I could see the sparkle of separate snowflakes on a wisp of her blond hair. We went into a theatre to see a play. On the program, among the names of those responsible for the production, was one name Marguerite recognized. During an intermission she said, "I want you to meet her. I knew her at the Neighborhood Playhouse."

We lingered after the final curtain, until nearly all the audience had gone out; and presently Marguerite saw this woman come into the large space back of the orchestra seats.

Her motion was quick and graceful, rather than gentle, and she had the air of walking alone, quickly, with a purpose, across the dark red carpet. She was a woman of average size—small to a tall man—but a woman of radiant force, to arouse a tall man's wonder. She was the living glow in that place of dim, ruddy light. Her face was warm, her eyes dark, and she had some grey in her dark hair.

We broke in on her isolation; and Marguerite introduced me to her. She frequently looked over her shoulder toward the stage and past us toward other people here and there whom she knew. She spoke in a low voice. We said nice things about the staging of the show, and she said nice things about seeing Marguerite again and meeting me. She looked up at me once, directly, for a moment, and appeared startled and then uneasy, as if she were used to being looked at for her appearance and her fame, but not for our tragic human quality of life. Though graceful, though yet in bloom, she was not young, but was already touched on the hands and on the throat and close beside the eyes by the fire-weaving of personal desire, which gives the flesh in youth a proud passionate splendor, but will at last burn out human beauty with lines of pain. Then the curtain was raised on after-the-play emptiness, and she looked professionally at the stage set. She said she had to go see about something she wanted to change—a matter of color contrast at stage right. This was spoken to us as if we could understand that she really had to go but as if we could not understand the priestly inwardness of the theatre which called her away. She excused herself with first a speculative and mistrustful glance at me, and then a final free and friendly smile at Marguerite. She went down the center aisle, probably quite sure that I was watching that swift, solitary way she moved. I though she was a lovely, self-engrossed woman, of Oriental fire, burning quiet.

I don't know, and never asked, whether at that time she and Wolfe were still in love or had broken off.

It was months later, in the spring of 1929, that I first heard Wolfe's name, prophetically spoken, in my living room.

One evening Marguerite and I gave a small party for some friends of ours. Among the guests were Byron Dexter, who then worked for the *New Republic,* and Alfred Dashiell, at that time assistant editor of *Scribner's Magazine,* both of them friends of mine since college days, and Wallace Meyer, who was in the book-publishing branch at Scribner's. My job then was editing a house organ for one of the Standard Oil companies. While Marguerite and the other women were talking domestic, we four men got onto the subject of books and authors. Fritz Dashiell asked me what I thought of the serial then running in *Scribner's Magazine*.

"Scant nourishment," I said.

"By" Dexter, who was hard-of-hearing, gave me an enquiring look, and I repeated the remark louder to him. He was amused, and asked what I considered nourishment in a book.

"The solace of tragic recognition."

By chuckled, and beaming at Fritz and Wallace, explained,

"Bob believes in the virtues. That's what comes of working for Standard Oil, and reading too much Conrad."

"You boys will grow up," I countered.

But Wallace Meyer, sitting on a straight chair, with his knees crossed, opened a copy of the magazine and pointed to a long paragraph in the serial, and said,

"Do you realize that whole paragraph is a single sentence? There is the whole record of a conversation in a single sentence a paragraph long. He'll work a whole morning in bed on a page like that, over and over, until it is just right. That's style!" Wallace handed me the magazine so that I could see for myself. He sat there as still as a young judge, fair, blue-eyed, wearing glasses with pale rims and earpieces. He did not seem excited, and yet he was about to utter a clear and surprising judgment. I can still remember with what certainty he spoke, as if the words could safely be cut in stone, for no revision would be necessary. He said.

"Hemingway is one of our two greatest writers."

"He and Willa Cather, or he and Sinclair Lewis?" I teased. "And what will we do about Theodore Dreiser?"

But Wallace's young and charming aplomb could not be shaken by a little slyness.

"No," he said, serious in the fullness of a great secret. "A man you never heard of. A book we're working on now. A first novel. It needs a lot of editing. It may be even greater than Hemingway, and very different. Fritz knows."

He let me look at Fritz Dashiell for confirmation. Fritz nodded his round, dark face soberly, and By Dexter, too, had the fulsome, shining look of a man who knew what was about to happen to American literature.

"What's the book? Tell me about it."

Wallace shook his head.

"We can't talk about it yet. The time hasn't come."

"What's the author's name? You can tell me that much."

"A man from down South. You'll hear about him next fall."

All this made the business of publishing sound important and mysterious; but I still had no idea of the man or the book.

Fritz gave one hint.

"I think you'll like the book, Bob. You like them eloquent."

Wallace Meyer summed the matter up,

"We're getting the book ready now. A great deal of it has to be cut, and at that it will be a long book. It's going to make a real noise when it's published." And with flush of fair cheeks and startled awe, he spoke foreknowledge of great things to come: *"Watch for the name of Thomas Wolfe!"*

Cornelia Dashiell called from the other end of the room,

"Are you talking about Tom Wolfe?"

"They're telling me to watch for his name next fall. Fritz says his writing is eloquent. That's not much to go on."

Cornelia, who was short, estimated my lean height with quick, dark eyes.

"You may think you're tall, Bob—but wait till you see Tom. He's six feet seven, and talks according."

I suppose while the publishers were working over his novel, cutting it down to market size, Wolfe had more than one moment of fear and hope. Would the first review of his book to reach him —the first sound of the public voice evoked by his labors and coming back to him—foretell fame or failure? How triumphant—or how tragic—is that first published word, of praise or of blame, that a young man reads about his first published novel! I forgot about this unknown writer, not dreaming that for him mine was to be the first public voice speaking of fame or of failure. For Thomas Wolfe it was to be my written word that would mark the end of being private and unknown and that would strike the first note of how the world at large might receive his work.

We moved to Beekman Place that summer, over by the East River, where tugs go snorting by with garbage scows. After some agreeable talk with Marguerite, I decided that, at the end of the year I would quit my job at Standard Oil, we would go live in Connecticut, and I would write books. Wolfe, hearing about this decision from Dashiell, long before he knew me, thought it bold and courageous. To establish this commitment to the hazard of becoming a writer for life, I began to review a few books for the *Herald Tribune* and for *Scribner's Magazine*. One day in September I went home from Scribner's office lugging a copy of *Look Homeward, Angel,* which Fritz Dashiell had asked me to review for their magazine. I spent three days reading it, and in two more finished my review of it.

Two and a half years later, in the first letter I received from Wolfe, he wrote:

That review was the first I read about my book. Max Perkins called me up one day and read it to me over the 'phone, and then I went out and walked about the streets in a great many different directions. I hope

I may have that feeling of jubilation and glory many times hereafter and that I shall always deserve as well and be treated as generously; but I know it will never again happen to me in just that way, because that was the first time and it could not be brought back . . .[1]

The review had also insulted him. He never told me this; but one night, out on a snow-covered hillside, seven years after the review was printed, Tom was doing some roaring in a bad mood, and by his vengeful use of one word from the review, I was able to understand what was eating him. Sometimes the continuance of a friendship depends upon what you do about a word.

[1] *Letters of Thomas Wolfe,* ed. Elizabeth Nowell, pp. 335–336.

2. THE LEGEND AND THE MAN

Marguerite and I went several times to Dashiell's house that winter, before we moved to the country; but Wolfe never happened to be there. Cornelia tried me in one of their doorways, which I could just pass through without scraping top, and assured me that Wolfe had to duck or bump his forehead.

Literary folk began to tell a story about Wolfe. I heard a few fanciful portions of it. We had moved to the country, where we had a small house beneath two elm trees; during 1930 I wrote *Brothers in the West,* which was published in August of 1931, and one result was that I met a few people interested in writing and in editing, publishing, reviewing, and selling the work of writers. Now and then one of them talked about Wolfe. For example, one day an assistant literary agent, a young fellow, who had curly hair and a lascivious tongue, began to talk about Thomas Wolfe. He talked as if he and Wolfe were old buddies, as if he and Tom were pals from the word go. He said he was looking forward to Wolfe's second book with hope-and-fear that he and other friends of his were going to be in it. Oh, he hoped the picture would not be too scandalous, the revelation too complete! I dare say he didn't make the grade; he was not included; and later he went to Hollywood; I shall therefore omit his name; but I am sorry to say that on one occasion, after midnight, in a white-top-table restaurant, I repeated a bit of his gossip to Wolfe, producing an awful effect.

The legendary Wolfe was in the making. Now and then there would be some item in the paper, perhaps an interview jeweled with a ridiculous anecdote to point out a gigantism. The literary folk, as the legend builders, did not, in regard to Wolfe, achieve that humane depth and good savor that the humble common man builds into his legends. It began to sound to me as if a lot of bright-minded, scant-hearted intellectuals thought here was a grotesque fellow sent to suffer in the world for their amusement. Thinking of *Look Homeward, Angel,* I realized, of course, that Wolfe had laid himself open to this torment by legend. But the general impression on one who had never met the man was fantastic.

Months would pass, however, during which I never thought about the legend or the man, and saw no literary folk, for I was writing another novel. Sometimes I wished I knew a few men nearby with whom I could talk about the quality of life in age old rather than in new deal terms. Marguerite would say,

"Bob, you don't know any authors your own size of devotion. You work alone. Why don't you go meet Mr. Wolfe? You can get Fritz to introduce you."

I thought this over, but, I confess, the legend repelled me. I am perhaps douce on top of dour, and would not wanton out of my way to join extravagance. Then one day in New York I stopped in at Scribner's office to say hello to Fritz. I asked him about Wolfe. Fritz shook his head with good Dutch sobriety and concern.

"Tom is having a hard time with his second book."

This was the touch that broke through the legend and pointed out a man; here was a writer, a worker, at labor on his second book, and having a hard time. God had made him oversize, from the heaven-rooted heart outward and from the earth-rooted toe inward; but God was not making it easy for any man to write a good book. When I got back to the country, I wrote a long letter to Wolfe saying, in effect, that I would like to make his acquaintance; and in a few weeks I got a long letter back from him saying he would like to get to know me.

I had the advantage of having read his book and the doubtful advantage of having heard the legend-making about him; Fritz had evidently told him something about me and he now realized I was the man who had written the first review of *Look Homeward, Angel* to reach him. I sent him a copy of *Brothers in the West* to even the matter up. Then one day in June, 1932, having set the date in an exchange of letters, I went in to the city to see him. He was then living at 111 Columbia Heights, Brooklyn. He expected me at seven o'clock in the evening.

I arrived at Burrough Hall shortly before six-thirty, it being my disposition to get to places ahead of time. I should have picked up a bite to eat, but I thought that as soon as I reached his place we would go out to dinner. Instead of eating, I ambled round about to his address, looked at buildings, looked at streets, looked at bridge towers, looked across the river at the towers of lower Manhattan with their irregular patterns of geometric aspiration. It was a mild evening, the ferocity of summer being yet in abeyance. It was five or ten minutes before seven when I rang the bell beside Wolfe's mailbox in the vestibule. The electric latch clicked and, opening the door, I began to climb stairs in a dark hallway, where ancient laziness or greed would let man stumble rather than provide a light. I was sorry so good an author as Wolfe had to reach his place of work and life up so sleazy a trench of dark.

As I reached the top of the flight to his floor, a door opened a crack, letting out light, and I heard a large, full, resonant voice rounding out a sentence. I liked the vigor, the manly music of that voice. Then the door opened wide.

Wolfe and I stood face to face for the first time.

I saw a giant young man with a moist forehead and dark disordered hair. My life is always on edge among my bones, like a hawk on a bare tree, and the wind rising. What he saw may have looked to him tall, lean, and dry. I think we did not like each other at first glance.

A little, short, skinny fellow was in the room behind him. I reached out my hand, saying,

"I am Bob Raynolds. Are you Mr. Wolfe?"

"Yes."

He let go of the doorknob and took my hand. As we shook hands we looked each other over the way one dog looks over another dog before they begin to play or fight.

"I'm glad to meet you, Mr. Raynolds. Come in. This is Mr. —."

He introduced me to the little black-haired man with the seamy, swart face, whose name I have forgotten. This nervous man was a teacher of history; he was cynical about his work and recollected people in terms of the humorous scandal he could repeat about them.

The room was plain, and was a workroom rather than a living room. The chairs were in bad condition, the bookshelves were in disorder, the lamps were crooked; but the ceiling was high, so that a man could pace the floor without feeling crowded down. Instead of assuming that Wolfe did not have enough money to rent more handsome quarters, I accepted it as a fact of his character that wherever he lived he would shake the place into disorder and not bother to set it right again.

I set my hat on a bookcase, and remained standing because Wolfe remained standing. He was firm on his feet; he carried himself well; and when he moved I saw that he was firm rather than agile. His lower eyelids had a slight fatness about them, couching his dark eyes in sensuous cradles of vigor and mirth. The truculence, the turbulence, and the pain were round about his mouth. His hair was black and he ran his fingers through it so that it usually looked shaggy. Because I am taller than most people I meet, it was pleasant, for a change, to meet a taller man than myself. He said to the other man,

"Mr. Raynolds has come down from Connecticut to have dinner with me."

"Are you an old friend of Tom's?" the teacher asked me.

"No. But I wanted to meet him, and asked if I could come. I'm a writer, too."

"Oh. What kind of stuff do you write?"

"I've had a novel published. I'm working on another."

"Mr. Raynolds' book got the Harper Prize last year," Wolfe explained. "He sent me a copy."

"Harper Prize! That's pretty good, isn't it?"

This three-cornered sparring for acquaintance was rather stiff; I thought a joke might help.

"Well, a lot of people think a prize proves something," I said. "But there's a good old Yankee lady up where I live. She belongs to a local book club; each lady buys a book, and then they pass the books around. She bought *Brothers in the West*, read it, and before sending it around to the other ladies, she wrote in it: 'I want it distinctly understood that this book is Harper's choice, not mine'."

The little man laughed. Wolfe had a quick look at my face, and when he saw by my grin that I enjoyed the story, he chortled. My guess was that he did not like people to make jokes about his work.

We all three sat down, in one of those masculine breathers that let the tongue go, though Wolfe frequently got to his feet again for a pace or two. The little man opened conversation about the university where he worked, about teaching-staff politics, and finally spoke of the treachery historians could embed in footnotes, which led him easily into some lewd anecdotes about the private lives of dead historians. At the door, as he was leaving, he recounted the vulgar grotesquerie by which a French historian got revenge upon an unfaithful mistress. He laughed, then sprang through the doorway and clattered down the steps—the merry exit of a jackanapes. I wanted to laugh and shout "Monkey!" after him.

Wolfe closed the door and looked at me. He had an idea that his pint-sized friend, just departed, might have offended me. But our mutual enjoyment of the ribald and the grotesque soon became one the strands of pleasure in our friendship.

"He's got a lewd tongue, but he's not as bad as he sounds, when you get to know him," he said, "I've known him quite a few years."

"He's a humorous cuss. I think he's alarmed at the scope of human nature, and runs to cynicism for comfort."

Wolfe leaned down to grab the back of a chair massively, and kicked the leg of it. "Look, Raynolds," he said—and this was the first time the "Mr." had been dropped between us—"I know enough about that fellow to know he's got kind feelings and wants his life to be good; yet all the time he was here, he didn't say a good thing about anybody. Why are so many young people bitter like that?"

"He's swallowed the destructive thinking of our so-called liberals and intellectuals. They produce no bread to live on and create no beauty of faith to live by, but they easily damn the working order of the world."

"You don't think the working order is good, do you? I've seen some terrible things in this Depression."

"The working order is balled up. But I think that the notion that society or government ought to provide a nontragic life for any one of us is a dream of ceasing to be men tragic and mortal."

It was eight o'clock. I was hungry. But we got to talking. There began to emerge the possibility of a limited friendship, based on a watchful adjustment between our antithetical natures. Dickens was the novelist he often spoke about, while I often spoke about Conrad—which tells our taste.

I told him I had liked *Look Homeward, Angel,* and thought especially that he had beat all other American authors at showing a small town's life. He told me of some of the vituperation his book had caused to be raised against him in his home town. Then I asked how he was getting on with his new book.

It was enough to do the writing, he said, without the additional burden of the literary crowd waiting, with animosity, for you to try to do it. His voice was troubled and his glance mistrustful, as if he thought I had come to leer at him. I gathered that specific curiosity tormented him. He was suspicious. This was a measure both of his pride and of the profound difficulty he was in. I knew he felt he had written *Look Homeward, Angel* in nakedness of spirit; but there was a more sombre quality in the mood that now for a moment darkened his face. He had to

> "Cleanse the stuff'd bosom of that perilous stuff
> That weighs upon the heart. . . ."

and no one had a right to question him about his progress. I asked no more about the work he was then doing. He could tell me when he wanted.

We discussed the matter of interviews, and the ease with which interviewers garbled what you said, reducing it to their own level of comprehension, making you sound like an ass. He showed me a couple of clippings to prove this point; and I told him about the woman from a Boston paper who had interviewed me, and then misrepresented me as saying that the modern woman had as much right to have children as she had to have an electric icebox. Again he gave me that swift glance to make out whether I was insulted or amused by such harebrained journalism. I think he found my amusement refreshing.

Then we got around to the question of whether or not an author knows how to describe things as they are, and he read me two passages introducing me to his two favorite and most alive horses in all the world. I had met both the horses before, but I liked meeting them again as he read them forth from their pages. The first horse paws in the Book of Job:

"Hast thou given the horse strength? hast thou clothed his neck with thunder? . . . He saith among the trumpets Ha! ha! and he smelleth the battle afar off, the thunder of captains, and the shouting."

Wolfe was a good reader; his ruddy round face and dark eyes glowed with fervor; he too was saying Ha! ha! among the trumpets. He tossed aside his small, use-battered Bible.

The other horse he said he loved cavorts in *Venus and Adonis:*

> "His eye, which scornfully glisters like fire,
> Shows his hot courage and high desire . . ."

But the point was, Wolfe challenged, could science better describe a horse than Shakespeare could? He read in his clear, melodious voice:

> "Round-hoofed, short jointed, fetlocks shag and long,
> Broad breast, full eye, small head and nostril wide,
> High creast, short ears, straight legs, and passing strong,
> Thin mane, thick tail, broad buttock, tender hide:
>   Look what a horse should have he did not lack,
>   Save a proud rider on so proud a back."

Wolfe was troubled, then, by the profound scientific bias of our age, which breeds contempt of the poet or the religious man. A writer, laboring for vision, feels this bias set against him at the top of each new page. See how Huxley considered a horse by his bones, while Job and Shakespeare struck to the life.

I agreed with Wolfe that these were marvelous steeds. The two horses I loved best were a dappled rocking horse with one broken foot, which I rode when I was five or six, and a little barrel of a shaggy, cinamon-colored Iceland pony which came into our family of children before I was seven. The horses I had ridden in Nebraska and Wyoming in my teens had generally been homely plugs that jogged my bones, and I had not much liked any one of them. I did not mention my various horses to Wolfe, my affections being humble and generally silent.

And yet, he said, plucking a heavy anthology from a heap of books, and reading to me the first paragraph from one of the shortest pieces in it, "Here's Huxley's autobiography, all told in a dozen pages. That's the way I wish I could tell my life."

I recollected my three-day's reading of *Look Homeward, Angel*, which was only the beginning of his story; and I looked at the packing case of manuscript on his floor and the welter of papers round about. I looked at him, standing there massive and aloft, his eyes bent on Huxley's clear, humorous, and audacious brevity. I began to laugh.

"Many's the time, Wolfe," I said, "when I have wished I could be a short, compact, close-coupled, energetic little fellow, striding hard and close to the earth in merry pleasure. And I guess I've got about as good a chance of waking up pudgy and comfortable as you have of writing your life in a dozen pages."

"Ha!" he said, and closed the book and slapped his thigh. "A million words, a thousand pages. Good God, Raynolds, I'm accursed! There's no end. This gigantic thing wells up in me like a storm."

" 'He stoppeth one of three'."

"That's a great poem. It had to be written. Coleridge had to write it. I've got to get this thing out of me or I'll choke to death on inner gorge."

Thus I found it was possible and pleasant to joke with him about his work, if the humor was open, direct, and friendly. He chuckled, he chortled, and his laughter came easily forth, when the humor was evolved from tragic recognition.

By nine o'clock when we stood up to go out to supper we were both informed of various personal matters: he was the taller and heavier man and eighteen months older than I; our racial heritage was similar—Scotch, Pennsylvania Dutch and English, though he had not my streak of Huguenot; we had both come originally from mountain country, he from among the green and smoky mountains of Carolina, and I from the desert foot of the Sangre de Cristo range in New Mexico; he was a bachelor, and I was married and the father of several children; he had warm, aware, brown eyes, while mine were sagebrush green with brown flecks.

My eyes looked sick to him less than an hour later.

3. HEAVING HIS TROUBLED TONGUE

We came out into the soft pleasant darkness of the small quiet street. Wolfe took a couple of sharp breaths of open air, as if it were a relief to him to get out of the room where he struggled with his work. "I've been writing all day," he said. "The air's fresh tonight." For a block no moving car passed us and only three or four were parked along the curbing; we were the sole pedestrians at that moment. Some lights were on in each of the brownstone-front houses, and a number of windows were alight in the modest apartment house across the street. Stars sprent the sky. Wolfe talked about the neighborhood, about living there, and about the larger subject of living in Brooklyn. I had begun to understand what Fritz Dashiell meant when he told me that Wolfe was a "wonderful talker."

He had a good way of walking along the street. He swung his long legs easily and his arms no more than needful; he carried his shoulders well; his torso was erect and firm and his head straight with innate dignity. In the parts of Manhattan and Brooklyn with which I was familiar (excepting Broadway at night) most people walked along the streets as if they were in a hurry to get to their business or in a hurry to get away from it; this gave their faces a set, cold look, harassed, secretive, prodded—bedevilled denizens of a soul-squeezing labyrinth. Wolfe walked along the street as if his business were right there; his business was to hear, see, feel, taste and touch and smell the life on the street; he was working as he walked. This gave his face an alert, lively expression, animal in its watchfulness, with his wary lower lip thrust out; then from time to time the gatherings of his senses coalesced in a spiritual perception, and the joy of spiritual apprehension lit up his face—"in apprehension how like a god."

We went along a dim street, then along another dim street to a speakeasy. We could hear an elevated train rumbling on Brooklyn Bridge. I had eaten nothing for nearly nine hours. We went down a few steps to the basement door of a brownstone house, and he rang the bell. A small curtain was pulled aside in a small window in the door, and a man looked out—just his face visible, three-quarters view, morbid and pale behind the little glass. He looked at where he expected to see the face of whoever had rung. They are usually not tall in Brooklyn. He saw the knot of my necktie and the top button of Wolfe's coat. (Wolfe seldom, if ever, wore a vest; either he bought suits without them, or used the vests to mend the pants.) Then the man tilted his head back, looked up at our faces, and grinned. He opened the door, cheerfully said, "Good evening, Mr. Wolfe!" and smiled at me.

"My friend and I would like a little something to eat and drink," Wolfe said.

There was a small bar straight ahead of us and to the right a small room crowded with small tables, and in both places some small people were eating and drinking.

We hung our hats on the hall rack and went into the room with tables. At this hour a number of the tables were empty. The men and women eating and drinking there looked at Wolfe on account of his extraordinary size, and then at me, because my head, too, moved up near the light globes in the low ceiling. We sat at a table for two, both of us sitting sidewise with our legs out into the room, for sitting opposite each other we could never both at once get our legs under the small table. The waiter dodged about our long legs and big feet.

"What'll you have to drink?" Wolfe asked me. "I've been here before. It's not so bad. They don't give you much food, but they have a good cook."

I was looking over the list of drinks. I didn't know which was which among cocktails; there was no speakeasy in Georgetown, Connecticut, where I spent most of my time. Wolfe said to the waiter, "I'll have a Martini," and I said, "Make it two." When the drinks came I saw by the color that they were gin drinks, and after that I remembered that Martinis were made with gin. We ordered a good dinner of broiled chops and, before it came, a second Martini each. We had only started eating when I felt cold and clammy, pulled my necktie loose, and asked where the men's room was. I had been absent less than five minutes when Wolfe was back there in the little white glare of the men's room asking how I was and was I all right? The two of us filled the cubicle.

"It must have been bad liquor," he said.

"I'm not used to drinking—and on an empty stomach—"

"You ought to get back to my room and lie down."

"I'll be all right. I'm sorry to get sick like this."

I wanted to pay for the dinner we hadn't eaten and the drinks we had drunk, but we ended by each paying half. I felt better, though weak, the minute we got outside into the cool, fresh air.

"Shall I get a taxi, Bob?"

"No, thanks, Tom. The walk will perk me up."

The crisis had brought us to first names.

We went back to his room. I lay on the bed muttering maledictions on my frailty, while Tom started a pot of coffee. The smell of the coffee was good. I had several cups and several slices of bread and butter. I began to feel good, though Tom said I still looked pale. Gradually his concern wore away and the extraordinary gentleness he had shown receded, its place being taken by what I would like to call his vivid creative interest in the subjects of conversation to which we addressed ourselves: writing, authors, people, how it was to be a man alive.

He spoke in a full-flowing resonant voice, down among the cellos, pleasant to hear, and, because of a continual variety in the stress, rhythm, and tune, easy to follow. (In the many years since his death I have often longed to hear his voice again.) The prime example of the literary man as talker seems to be Coleridge. Many people have written about Coleridge the Talker. From what I have read, I gather that Coleridge could take a large subject, preferably philosophical or mystic, and boom along about it by the hour. Tom admired Coleridge, his great power of speech and rare poetic power. I said I was impressed by the life Coleridge could get out of plain small words, and taking a volume from one of the shelves I read:

> "The fair breeze blew, the white foam flew,
> The furrow followed free;
> We were the first that ever burst
> Into that silent sea . . ."

"He was a great prose writer, too," Tom said. "I think a good poet can always write good prose." He reached for the book from my hand, thumbed among its pages, and then, standing firm on his feet with his body swinging about in a slight circle, he read the fragment about Cain, beginning: "A little further, O my Father, yet a little further, and we shall come into the open moonlight."

As the night deepened and our talk went on I realized how different Wolfe was from Coleridge as a talker. If Coleridge was a literary talker of great power, fluttering his opiate tongue to make drowsy, mystic music, Wolfe was a commonplace talker of great power, heaving his troubled tongue to unbury the fire of common life: a man, a street, a place, a time.

He sat now in one chair, now in another, his necktie at first untied, then cast off; he smoked cigarets; he listened. He was more inclined to put his right ankle on his left knee (gripping his right foot in his large left hand) than he was to cross his knees, which is my parlor commonplace. Sometimes the smoke of his cigaret curled up past the clear-cut tip of his straight nose. There was something about the precision, placement, and proportion of his nose that gave his face a leonine aspect—of a young lion still in the smoothness of rising power. My aquiline face was not yet burnt so dour as it would become later. He crushed out cigarets in the saucer of his coffee cup; he poured fresh coffee for us both from the percolator. I had a couple of pipes with me and smoked one of them, then the other. He told me about Burton's *Anatomy of Melancholy,* and in return I told him about Doughty's *Arabia Deserta,* which was a good trade in mental backlogs.

He asked questions, too: "Do you think two hundred dollars a month is too much for a writer to live on? Do you think I should go to Hollywood? Do you think I ought to get out of Brooklyn?" He told me, without naming her, about a woman he had known a while ago. "She was connected with the theatre, but she always went to books for her allusions: 'Wrap up warm, Nancy.' I guess it was love, if a woman would come to my rooms, again and again, to cook for me. God, she could make a meal!—Do you think a man has to go all the way to Spain to find out about death?"

I did not get the name, shape, or nature of the book he was writing from any specific thing he said: some authors can tell you they are working on a book of twenty chapters in outline as follows; but Wolfe, I could see, was an eloquent apologist, and the lives of the great apologists do not come in balanced chapters or by outline. Moreover, he was not serene: his glance was alarmed and vivid, his voice was troubled, his physical motions were spasmodic and wary; evidently he was laboring through a spiritual crisis, more like a war than a battle.

About three A.M. I said I'd better leave, because I was staying overnight at my mother-in-law's apartment (breakfast at eight). We shook hands at the door, saying we hoped we would meet again.

"I'd like to have you come out to Georgetown. A weekend, or during the week, if you prefer. Marguerite would be pleased, too."

"I'm in the midst of work now."

"Sometime when you're sick of it, let me know."

On the subway platform, solitary, in a chill draft and hollow sort of cold, I thought about the meeting, the man, and the parting. Between three and four o'clock in the morning trains rumble rarely along the subway tunnels. I walked back and forth, the only waiting passenger, or sometimes leaned against a post. Wolfe was friendly; he was gentle; he was densely webbed of earth and fertile, like a field where God's bread is grown.

I got back to the country, tired, the next evening. Marguerite, an eloquent teller of her adventures, wanted to hear all about mine.

"Did you like him?"

"Yes."

"Tell me about him."

"I got sick and he took care of me."

"What's he like?"

"He is a big man. He talks. He is homeless."

"When will you see him again?"

"I don't know."

4. THE WEB OF EARTH

He never came to see me in Georgetown. I wrote, inviting him to come, perhaps several times, and he meant to come once in mid-summer; but when I met the train, he was not on it. I thought this over, and concluded he was in some sort of trouble of his own, that his failure to turn up as agreed was not meant as an affront. I went to New York seldom that summer; I was busy finishing *Saunders Oak*; but, without seeing Wolfe again, I got to know him better by thinking about him.

He traipsed about the landscape of day and night, with fire in his shoes, hunting after himself; and he dwelt in the midst of fury.

His ambition was monstrous; he was not merely intent upon survival or upon making a comfortable and modest way in the world; he had come up to the city with an impassioned ambition to achieve splendor; he roved the streets of the day and the night to garner the materials of glory, and spilled the torrents of his gathering into a thousand pages, meanwhile still gathering more, hoping more, and awaiting the crown of the world. The cobra of the world was at his heart. It is no light thing for a man of great mind and powerful imagination to seek peace and glory in the world. In a book Wolfe loved to read, Burton's *Anatomy of Melancholy,* the great snake of human misery coils with comic and terrible majesty; see the motion and virulence of but one sliding sentence of that work:

In a word, the world itself is a maze, a labyrinth of errors, a desert, a wilderness, a den of thieves, cheaters, etc., full of filthy puddles, horrid rocks, precipitiums, an ocean of adversity, an heavy yoke, wherein infirmities and calamities overtake and follow one another, as the sea waves; and if we scape Scylla, we fall foul of Charybdis, and so in perpetual fear, labor, anguish, we run from one plague, one mischief, one burden to another, *duram servientes servitutem* (undergoing a hard bondage), and you may as soon separate weight from lead, heat from fire, moisture from water, brightness from the sun, as misery, discontent, care, calamity, danger, from man.

Reading this book, which I had bought because Wolfe spoke of it at length, I thought of Burton as a great comic writer, himself hugely enjoying every page he wrote; but he wrote with a scholar's dry security; whereas Wolfe wrote in the anguish of spiritual crisis. I had to go to St. Augustine to find one who knew the intimate coils and present fangs of the cobra of the world as Wolfe knew them, for one who, like Wolfe, could celebrate the intensity and agony of sensuous life with words out of his heart.

O madness, which knowest not how to love man, like men! [St. Augustine laments his lost friend, as in his depths Thomas Wolfe lamented his lost self]. O foolish man that I then was, enduring impatiently the lot of man! I fretted then, sighed, wept, was distracted; had neither rest nor counsel. For I bore about a shattered and bleeding soul, impatient of being borne by me, yet where to repose it, I found not. Not in calm groves, not in games and music, nor in fragrant spots, nor in curious banquetings, nor in the pleasures of the bed and of the couch;

nor in books or poesy, found it repose. All things looked ghastly, yea, the very light; whatsoever was not what he was, was revolting and hateful, except groaning and tears. For in these alone I found a little refreshment. But when my soul was withdrawn from them, a huge load of misery weighed me down. To Thee, O Lord, it ought to have been raised, for Thee to lighten; I knew it; but neither could nor would; the more, since, when I thought of Thee, Thou wast not to me any solid or substantial thing. For Thou was not Thyself, but a mere phantom, and my error was my God. If I offered to discharge my load thereon, that it might rest, it glided through the void, and came rushing down again on me; and I had remained to myself a hapless spot, where I could neither be nor be from thence. For whither should my heart flee from my heart? Whither should I flee from myself? Whither not follow myself? And yet I fled out of my country, for so should mine eyes look for him, where they were not wont to see (him). And thus from Thagaste I come to Carthage . . .

Thus Wolfe had fled out of his home to Boston, from Boston to New York, thence to Europe, to New York, to Europe and finally (as he had written me), "goaded by necessity and desperation I came to Brooklyn."[2] Each of them, St. Augustine and Thomas Wolfe, still sought in the world the image of consolation, however different in the end might be their findings. I could open *Look Homeward, Angel* and find on the first page:

O waste of loss, in the hot mazes, lost, among bright stars on this most weary unbright cinder, lost! Remembering speechlessly we seek the great forgotten language, the lost lane-end into heaven, a stone, a leaf, an unfound door. Where? When?
O lost, and by the wind grieved, ghost, come back again.[3]

Still, there was a kind of innocence of accomplishment in this first telling of his story; but the second book he was writing was coming harder than the first, with the anguish more present and

---

[2] *Letters of Thomas Wolfe*, pp. 335–336.
[3] *Look Homeward, Angel,* Epigraph.

terrible. *Look Homeward, Angel* had not set him free; it had embroiled him deeper and set him more sharply at peril. I think my own knowing of this same sort of thing deepened my compassion for the overwrought spirit of my new and absent friend.

We had exchanged several friendly letters during the summer; in September I went to see him again. He had moved a few doors along the street.

I crossed Brooklyn Bridge at evening, afoot, from where the bridge stoops down among a scrabble of foul old buildings on Manhattan, over and up above the river and the boats, where the wind blew and the city was a vision, to where the bridge stoops down among a foul scrabble of old buildings in Brooklyn. (I have not been on the Bridge since Tom left Brooklyn, and perhaps things have changed in these many years.) I stopped at a grimy, white-fronted eat shop for a hot dog and a glass of cold blue milk, thus fortifying myself against the long wait for supper and a probable drink before eating. As I munched my food I looked speculatively at the anemic girl in a food-spotted, white waitress' dress who had served me. She was leaning her buttocks against the edge of a three-well ice-cream bin back of the counter, to take the weight off her feet, drowsing in some sort of dream of rest, with that tired stare of the hard-beaten at the end of the day. She had a pinched nose, a frail throat, and her narrow arms were folded under her meager breasts. I laid my money on the counter and said,

"I'm on my way to see a friend who calls Brooklyn a jungle."

First she twisted her mouth, then focused her eyes on me, became reassured, cheered.

"God! He said it! Jungle!" She smiled, taking to heart a poet's word for her dwelling place. "I'll remember that. Jungle!"

Instead of turning right, through the prosperous regions of Pierrepont Street, I took the sinister way to Tom's door, going down past blackened windows and shut doors and closed-out shops, close to the smell of the river. Near one corner in the dusk I saw a lean man in a black coat, stooped like a hollow-bellied dog over a garbage can at the curb, selecting food. He paid no attention to me as I passed him and swung left, up a short hill, with a view askance at the splendid, lofty, and slender towers of Lower Manhattan.

The latch in the vestibule at Wolfe's new address was loose; I went in, climbed the stairs, and knocked on his door.

He yanked the door open and stood back; he had a look in his eye tigerish, and in the ball of his right thumb the groove of anguish, furrowed there by gripping his pencil in the fierce joy of writing. His shirt collar was torn wide open to ease the broad base of his throat for the dithyrambic rush and throb of his blood, which redded his face, and his nostrils flared wide, sucking in oxygen to stoke the creative fires of his creative, massive breast. The complete and gentle politeness with which he recognised me and said, "Come in, Bob," made more astounding and vivid the flush of power in which he was at work. I knew that no one could enter an author's presence while he was at work without violating his processes.

"I'll sit here in horrid silence, gnawing away at the base of your brain, while you make a mess of finishing what I've interrupted."

Some satiric flash in my words or tone lessened the shock of my intrusion. He gave me an explosive, joyous glance, then turned his back on me, went to his table, which was a battlefield of yellow paper scattered; he leaned over, his left hand flat on a batch of writing, the weight of his torso on his left arm, and he finished writing the page with the wild ease of a Cossack cutting another enemy down to the ground. If I had not come just then, he might have slaughtered two and twenty demons, instead of one, through the lone night.

He straightened up and turned to face me. "Thanks for letting me finish. I'm getting some sections together."

"Patching up the sore gaps left by creative editing?"

"I started to do a few pages about a miserable little fellow I knew; but I got going, and it was twenty thousand words, and Perkins says the book won't stand it. God, they cut my heart out!"

I had sat sidewise in the easy chair with the broken springs; my back was against one arm of the chair and my legs dangled over the other arm. I was smoking my pipe, and looked up at him while he lit a cigaret. He stood there legs apart, vibrant, his face flushed, his black hair in a muss, his eyes sparkling with insatiate lust for the world; he took a deep first drag on the cigaret, then blew a cloud of smoke out about his head.

"A man writes," Tom said, "and he sets down something with his heart's blood, and then it gets cut out."

"I know an editor who thinks Rabelais is wordy, and that *War and Peace* and *Moby Dick* could be improved no end by shrewd cutting. The insight of editors amazes me!"

Rays from the two lamps lit up whorls of smoke from his cigaret and my pipe; these whorls of smoke curled and shifted up and down in sinuous unrest; and he looked at me through these whorls of smoke intently, speculatively; then his warm, round face relaxed, a smile thawed the pain out of his mouth, and pleasant mirth fattened the corners of his eyes.

"Ha!" he said, tossing his head in the midst of the smoke. "It's the greatest thing in the world to be a writer!"

And we fell to talking shop. To escape suffering, many authors, after a while on the wrack, go on piecework, like other factory hands, turning out a saleable article; and their shop talk is about cents-per-word, contracts, story markets, agents, magazine merchandise, the Hollywood angle, etc. We talked rather about how to bridge the gap between the heart and the word, between the life and the image, or about the wages paid to Chatterton, Keats, Van Gogh, and old seamy-faced Rembrandt. These extreme tortures Tom was receiving on his second book did not impress me as unmerited; they were simply the just wages of willfulness, the rate of pay established by the gods for poets, creators. These are the wages of Prometheus, and Tom had the pride and joy of Prometheus in his face.

It was a long conversation, dropped and resumed; the days and the seasons passed; we talked; he labored at his second book; he may already have been on the third or fourth or fifth telling of his story; but it would come out to the public, some day, as the second telling: *Of Time and the River.*

And meantime, as those seasons passed, and I saw Tom often, I injured my back skiing, which put a blight on my physical life and shoved my spirit further into solitude; I finished writing *Saunders Oak*; we moved from Georgetown some fifteen miles to a more roomy house in Newtown, where, on account of the new fragility of my back, I could do little about the place, nor could I toss the three children, now at the age for tossing, so that they missed a good part of a father, and so did I; I went on a brief lecture tour; *Saunders Oak* was published about the time I spoke in Cleveland; the bank holiday caught me in the monstrous confines of the Hotel Stevens in Chicago; and Tom and I ate together in Brooklyn or Manhattan, then returned to his room to talk out a winter's night or a summer's night.

Politics was a paragraph in our long discourse; neither of us was Aristotle's political animal; each of us was more like the poet thrown out of Plato's Republic. My comments in the political paragraph were the more conservative, Tom's the more liberal, but neither of us had the fight or the fanatacism of the ideological man; we had a similar sense of the human ground, upon which politics is a variable excresence, and because of our agreement concerning the tragic essence of the human ground, we never annoyed each other by differences in matters politic.

Day in and day out around us there was an immense dissatisfaction with the management of the world, and an increased worship of the power principle of managing it. If you just handled God aright—in fact, if you just took His place, with your own set of blueprints, and spent the money and gave the orders and increased your power, presto! the abundant life would rain upon the forgotten man. The true national seat of will, license, and the pursuit of power, having been snatched from Wall Street on the Hudson, was now being re-reared under alphabetical aegis beside the broad Potomac. These great changes in the seat of power and the angle of its abuse in no way amended the wickedness of mere power; malice was large about, hate fast breeding. Nor had this new political fatness (which made spiritual society lean) in any way lightened for Wolfe the tribulation of searching insatiate for peace in glory; it had lightened not the agony of trying to find, in the white blaze of what he called "Absence," the integrity of his soul.

Getting up from ten thousand words, with the pencil groove bruised in his thumb and graphite smeared on the ball of his hand, and going out onto the streets of day and night, he saw hunger, he heard anger, and by the faces of men he knew that the lie of self-interest was still spawning new anguish in common hearts. Still the world snapped out snares of interthreading fire at the tower of his brain, sending new lures and fresh-faced glories, flanked and bottomed by old corruption, to storm the central citadel of his spirit. There had been another Thomas (an old friend of his and mine) who knew such battle. "The Devill that did but buffet Saint Paul, playes meethinkes at sharpe with me: let me be nothing if within the compasse of myselfe, I doe not find the batell of Lepanto, passion against reason, reason against faith, faith against the Devill, and my conscience against all."

In his Brooklyn room, so lorn a place, or after midnight on the streets of Manhattan, hard and terrible in night silence, like very canyons of sterile death, when we two men walked together alive, he told me his dreams were sore; he told me that rumor wounded his name; and he would laugh with Lear's Fool: "Tom's a-cold!"— and then say to me gravely what Hamlet, dying, said to Horatio:

> "O good Horatio, what a wounded name,
> Things standing thus unknown, shall live behind me!
> If thou didst ever hold me in thy heart,
> Absent thee from felicity awhile,
> And in this harsh world draw thy breath in pain,
> To tell my story."

Slabs of his work got in print before the book appeared. Once, when we paused at the corner of Forty-seventh Street and Sixth Avenue to wait for the traffic lights to change before crossing under the dark, lank trestle of the elevated railroad (I don't think he lived to see it torn down) I warned him, saying,

"Tom, you're laying the skids under *Scribner's Magazine*. A few more pieces like 'The Web of Earth,' or 'Portrait of Bascome Hawk,' or 'Death the Proud Brother,' and that magazine will be on the rocks. I know you're not doing it on purpose, you don't want to make Fritz hunt another job, but I can't believe any American magazine can publish literature and survive."

It was a late spring afternoon, with mild, gritty air, and bunches of dingy, hunger-faced men stood in depressed knots in front of the doors of employment joints, looking at the cards posted there calling for waiters, railroad hands, night men, porters, and others for dull labor. There Tom stood, towering above them, legs apart and feet firm, his body rotating, his eyes alight, and laughter chortling out of his throat in good warm gurgles, like mulled wine out of a flagon.

(*Scribner's Magazine* soon folded up and faded out, and our mutual friend, Fritz Dashiell, went onto the staff of the *Reader's Digest*, which does not toy with the great long song of literature.)

Then Tom looked at the tired moil of men by the doors of the employment joints, their eyes raised and their mouths open for crumbs of work, and his face got truculent, fierce, and dark.

"All over America in little towns," he said, "boys dream of the City. A boy dreams of the splendor and magnificence of the City, and comes here with his brain burning with expectant fire; and he sees a thousand nameless men misery-drugged in batches like these."

There they were, a blotch on his dream, clustering, moving, one going away with his hands pocketed and his head wrung down, another edging in with a moistening of lips, in front of these dark doorways, in front of the dirty shopwindows full of junk, pornography, cheap hardware; stunted men, scant-shaven, bitter-faced, ten to a job, waiting for something to be posted that would make it worth while to work instead of stay on relief. This was the City of Man, so splendid in the dreams of a boy, and when found— behind the flower face of a mistress, outside the warm welcome of editorial offices, beneath the towering glory of the sun-smote buildings where men had made millions for yachts and baubles—these knots of slump-footed men, a blotch on the dream, a true dread pain in the heart.

He was hurt and angered by the pain and condition of men.

We crossed when the lights favored us, and went on toward Fifth Avenue. And his own work troubled him. He was talking as we walked along the street, giving his big right hand an extra strong wide swing now and then, as it were the hand of Samson flaying out with the jawbone of an ass. The second book was hard a-borning. Sure, great fragments of it were turning up in *Scribner's Magazine*: he could eat on that. But a woman had flung much matter awry: threats of lawsuit if this were published, threats of suicide if that were included. Who was writing the book, anyway? And where and when was the end? For there was the matter of length, breadth, thickness, form.

"What a man writes is form. But they want exact little books, from here to there, and no fat of life larded in between. I can't stop myself: today is part of the book I was writing yesterday. I remember everything; I forget nothing, and it all belongs to the book. Good God, I'm writing a library."

"Take 'The Web of Earth'," I said. "That has form. It has form and motion. It has the rise and fall of a great wave. No American before you knew how to write a story like that. Motion is part of your form, just as it is part of America's form, and that's why your books have too large a swing for easy minds to grasp."

I glanced at him, striding beside me in the sun, one button of his coat closed tight across his belly, and wondered if anyone ever saw Thomas Wolfe when he was not in motion? If you drop a piece of sodium into water, it will scurry and spurt about, giving off heat and light till it is done for; so Thomas Wolfe, dropped into the fluid midst of mankind, was speeding to and fro and around amongst us, flashing out heat and light. "And he'll do it till he's consumed," I thought. "He's a religious poet, chaunting of Hell, and he'll probably burn up before he gets round to Purgatory or Paradise."

This was one of those momentous thoughts that rise in the mind without thinking, and require afterthought to be understood. I considered the long swing and stroke of his work. Its amplitude did not interest me much: quantity is bootless in a world wanting vision. But the man was in motion: "The Web of Earth" was a move beyond *Look Homeward, Angel*; he might live his way through and out of this hellish, isolating pain of self-absorption, which compelled him to personal seizure of the moment to glut his self; he might yet move on to the grand calm of humane vision, which a few great artists have achieved. I saw more in the good live man beside me than had yet appeared in his work. I knew by now that much of his talking, focused by extra labor and fringed with poetic fire, became pages of his book; but when he talked there was often a lift, a joy, a yeast of hope, that he lost when he wrote it down; when he came to write it down, he was apt to add words like "ruined," "lost," "sorrowful," "lonely," "fury," "agony," "madness," "death," as if he steeped in some deep, subconscious pool of hell whatever he saw or remembered, before he could give it back in writing. Yet the man labored for heaven with the energy of an Augustine. I think I foresaw, even then, for an instant, the hazard of soul that lay before him and the hazard of death that might cut him off before fulfillment. I was startled to apprehend in a living man beside me the presence of that human grandeur which words cannot scope and which no man fulfills, but which, in the great, shows forth in prophecy of the human possible.

The weight and urge of our disjointed time, with its praise of scathing and hatred, was against him. But he was haunted by Time and by a dream which the world of the passing day could not fulfill; he was moved by the deep, internal sweep of old anxiety and by primal human longings; he was a religious man. He might rise out of this present wild young frenzy of the cosmic martyr to the clear vision and hopeful utterance of a healed and humble man. The great good beauty of his toiling life and of his mortal peril often, in his presence, moved me to a compassion which deepened my heart.

Then again, at night, having bruised and scraped our knees on the seats in front of us at a theatre, we were returning to Brooklyn. We came into the elevator in the St. George Hotel; there were no other passengers; the Negro operator, who was not more than five feet tall, closed the door, then turned and tilted back his head to look up at us. He had a horsey, fifty-year-old face with something grey in its furrowed blackness, and grey in his woolly hair.

"You two is sure big men," he said. He started to push the lever, thought better of it, and looked up at us again. "The Lord, He didn't economize on length when he made up you two gentlemen."

"My friend here is six-feet three," Tom said.

"And my friend is taller than the walls of Jericho," I added.

The Negro grinned bright and wide.

"A thin one, like the gee-raffe, and a thick one, like the ely-phunt; sure the works of the Lord are wonderful!"

We went on to an Armenian restaurant Tom knew, to eat little chunks of lamb on a spit. There we saw a little wretch making a buffoon of himself, after midnight, to cadge a drink from fellows who spurred him on with wisecracks at his misery. I said it reminded me of the buffoons who turn up, soul-sick and smote with divinity, in the novels of Dostoevski; and Tom said that Alyosha, in *The Brothers Karamazov*, was perhaps the most wonderful figure in any novel he knew. But the center of his mind, day in and day out, was on his own work.

Another night, near that great sterile and dingy public building, Burrough Hall, we sat in a vast, bright restaurant—"food factory," Tom called it—and amid the noise and bustle each of us ate a goodly plank steak ringed with vegetables, and floated it awash down to our bellies with beer. He must have had a tough time that day at the grasping of images and the slaughter of pages, for his eyes glared truculent over his food and round the swarming room. He muttered that he had lived too long in Brooklyn, the jungle.

Then we came out onto the street of night, with its hard small
lights aglister and the men and women of Brooklyn trudging the
dirty glitter of their jungle pathways. He stuck out his lower lip,
full, cherry dark, and puffed with anger, whirled his great arms
straight out sidewise from his heavy shoulders, so that his arms
swept swift and terrible over the heads of the swarming men and
women of Brooklyn.

"Runts!" he cried. "Runts!"

The second book was hard indeed a-borning.

We were sitting in his room, perhaps late in the sulky summer
night, drinking coffee from his generous pot. His tie was off, his
shirt open, his fingers moiled his thick black hair, anguish was on
his lip and wild pleasure in his fervid eyes. He handed me a thin
book that had three stories in it about men in blue suits.

"Read the one about me."

There were books and batches of typescript and manuscript on
shelves and in a big wooden box on the floor; on the table were
scatterings of cheap yellow paper scrawled over in pencil, sometimes not more than a sentence flung down aslant on a page, sometimes a spate from top to bottom. Tom lay on a couch at one end
of the room, smoking, glaring at the ceiling, and watching me
like a sharp cat; I stood up and walked about, turning the pages
of the little story. Finally I tossed the book aside.

"It may be about you, Tom; but she hasn't caught your rumble.
The doe in the woods whimpers of Niagara Falls, but she makes
only a little sound of herself."

"She sent it to me. She can publish that, and then go faint on
the floor at Scribner's office to prevent me from getting out my
writing. Stark Young happened to be there, and told her she was
being too theatrical about it."

"She stuffs a baggy blue suit with suet and straw, to assuage some bewilderment fretting her own heart; but your lusty vehemence is not in it."

He snorted bitterly and smoked and glared at the ceiling. There he lay on the couch at one end of the room, glaring at the ceiling, probably riven by pangs of fury and loneliness, made more bitter and acute by my strange presence; then he rolled his head sidewise for a slant stare at me, and I could see that his intense, concentrated, and potent creative lust was not adrowse; it sparked, the tiger of his soul, round about the jungle corners of his eyes, ready to pounce on whatsoever might be, for his spirit, the meat of the moment and matter passing. And at the other end of the room lay pages in his swift writing of the book not yet finished; it might be that among them were these fresh words:

He never knew; but now mad fury gripped his life, and he was haunted by the dream of time. Ten years must come and go without a moment's rest from fury, hungering, all of the wandering in a young man's life. And for what? What?[4]

Or it may have been these words, stirring in the deeps of his mind, which became the mature testament of his labor and his life:

From the beginning—and this was one fact that in all my times of hopelessness returned to fortify my faith in my conviction—the idea, the central legend that I wished my book to express had not changed. And this central idea was this: the deepest search in life, it seemed to me, the thing that in one way or another was central to all living was man's search to find a father, not merely the father of his flesh, not merely the lost father of his youth, but the image of a strength and wisdom external to his need and superior to his hunger, to which the belief and the power of his own life could be united.[5]

He lay there on the couch, wakeful, watchful, prodigious with

[4] *Of Time and the River*, p. 91.
[5] *The Story of a Novel*, p. 39.

life, as Michelangelo's Adam might lie roused on the rock of the world yet a moment after God had smote him through the fingertip with the fire and fury of life. And for a moment there in the room with him, I had forgotten him and his works, being vivid and joyous with an apprehension of my own; so that when our eyes met again, we were both startled, as two men coming forth from opposite wildernesses and separate solitude for a chance meeting on human ground.

And to lighten his sorrowed sense of laboring alone and forgot in the wilderness of the world, I took from my inside pocket a paper on which I had written, and handed it to him.

"See if you think it's all right. I wrote it a few days ago."

He unfolded the sheet, read it, smiled, and was pleased. This is what I had written:

On Thomas Wolfe

His magic pencil's living poise and slide,
>   By late lamplight, across the tablet's face,
>   Has won from wilderness a giant race,
And all the secrets of their hearts descried;
Or did some Angel stoop and long confide
>   Into his humble ear the runs of grace
>   Whereby this miracle has taken place
Of forming men from words put side by side?
Morelike, this troubled organ flow of sound,
>   This lusty music of a Titan breast,
In which a "Web of Earth" has fitly found
>   Its spokesman wrapt with ecstacy, was wrest
In long, lone turmoil from the dark profound
>   Where mind and heart and soul secrete their best.

After he and I had taken our trip to the piddling mountains of Vermont, after my wife and I and one of my daughters (all innocently) had insulted him, after his revenge on a New Year's Eve, and after our friendship had survived that crisis, I had this sonnet published on the dedication of *Fortune*, my third novel.

5. THE LOST BOY

The evening was over, but the night was young. I paced back and forth on the sidewalk in front of Scribner's offices on Fifth Avenue, waiting for Wolfe, who was upstairs doing some work with Perkins. I had never seen Perkins; I wondered what he was like. The homegoing traffic had dwindled; the theatre traffic had not begun; the Avenue and the sidewalks were quiet. Presently Wolfe burst out of the door and stood tremendous on the walk. We shook hands. He gave his hatbrim an extra tug, then he turned, put his hands on his hips, bent back his head, and looked up at a lighted window on the fourth or fifth floor, which was Perkins' office window.

"Ha!" he said. "Perkins is a wonderful man. Perkins is a wonderful man, Bob."

We started walking down the Avenue.

"At least, he knows a dithyramb when he sees one," I said.

"I just showed him a big piece I've written. He reads it. He tips back his hat. He looks at me with his sea-pale eyes. He says, 'It's good, Tom.' I say, 'Listen, Max. I'm going crazy. When am I going

to finish this book?' He tugs his ear, says, 'Not yet, Tom.' 'By God,
Max, it's my sweat and blood.' 'Keep on,' he says, 'you're doing fine.'
I tell you, he's a wonderful man. He knows what I'm doing. By
God, I wish I knew myself. I'll never finish. Tonight or tomorrow
I'll remember something else that's got to go in."

We were licking up the sidewalk in our long strides. We swung
across Forty-fifth Street, and went toward Broadway.

"Memory is endless, and insufficient," I said.

"If a man could remember the beginning. When was the instant
of life? Where? What? It's in a man's memory, if he could find it."

"I like the first four words of the Bible, Tom. They comfort me."

He was a huge-memoried man. He knew his remembrance of
life was remarkable, and he spoke of it with pride.

"It's like chaos and old night and like the deep and backward
abysm of time, and works with the yeast of sea life and soil life. It's
a terrible monster, burgeoned on my guts. It knows all, all!"

When he wrote "The Web of Earth," he celebrated a like en-
dowment in his Mother.

Remember! Now, boy, you ask me if I can remember! Lord, God!
. . . I can remember all the way back to the time when I was two years
old, and let me tell you, boy: there's mighty little I've forgotten since![6]

We turned into a barroom for a drink before dinner. As we
entered the door, he said,

"If a man could remember the beginning— Why life?"

It was one of those low-ceilinged barrooms, with oily dark wood-
work. In a room visible beyond the bar a few people were having
dinner. No one was drinking at the bar when we came in. We
ordered Old Fashioneds.

I said that of course I knew, from hearsay, a number of things
about my childhood, but I doubted if I had actual personal mem-

[6] In *From Death to Morning*, pp. 214–215.

ory, on a conscious level, of any impressions received before I was about five years old. He said he could do better than that.

We stirred our drinks with the glass rods. Tom gripped his glass hard and firm in his big hand, took a sip, set it down hard, stared into the mirror. "I can remember from the time I was a baby in a basket on the porch; I can remember the sunlight on the porch, and my sister going up the hill toward school. And I can remember St. Louis, when I was three years old, getting on four. Some day I'm going back to the house there; I'll find something."

Tom squeezed his glass in his great hand as if to squeeze the juice of life out of it, took a long drink, smacked his lips, and said, "I remember how my father used to roar and rend the household air with fulgent psalms of wrath, as readily if a fly buzzed as if someone's evil deed stalked his brain; it was because he loved life. You see a woman, and you remember a thousand women. I've written to Mama for the exact location of that house in St. Louis. It's important. Someday I'll go there, to the house, to the room, and I'll find something. But you can't go home again. You can't find your father again."

"Home is forward in my geography. I've never been there yet."

He considered my face a moment. We drained our glasses and ordered a second drink. There was a shadow of sombre thought on his face; then he shook his head. My spiritual geography was not for him; we were different fellows indeed; we drank a while in silence. There was no hope in his ambition, because it was like a vengeance, involving all the toil and salt reward of vengeance. He was attuned to violence; his moments of rising exultation ended again and again in the shock of horror; in his writing, brute catastrophe and insensate death broke off motion; and still he sought in his labyrinthine memory some magic, lovely, and changeless image of peace; a hope of fulfillment, of revelation, lay secreted in some memory before disaster.

It was a matter of such importance that he wrote his mother at least three times for the address of that house in St. Louis, and finally reaching St. Louis, hunted up the house, to see if he could find, in a room where he had been a small child, the integrity of his soul. He wrote about this journey to this shrine:

And he felt that if he could only sit there on the stairs once more, in solitude and absence in the afternoon, he would be able to get it back again. Then he would be able to remember all that he had seen and been—the brief sum of himself, the universe of his four years, with all the light of Time upon it—that universe which was so short to measure, and yet so far, so endless, to remember. Thus would he be able to see his own small face again, pooled in the dark mirror of the hall, and peer once more into the grave eyes of the child he had been, and discover there in his quiet three-year's self the lone integrity of "I," knowing: "Here is the House, and here House listening; here is Absence, Absence in the afternoon; and here in this House, this Absence, is my core, my kernel—here am I!"

But as he thought it, he knew that even if he could sit here alone and get it back again, it would be gone as soon as seized, just as it had been then—first coming like the vast drowsy rumors of the distant enchanted Fair, then fading like cloud shadows on a hill, going like faces in a dream—coming, going, coming, possessed and held but never captured, like lost voices in the mountains long ago—like the dark eyes and quiet face of the dark, lost boy, his brother, who, in the mysterious rhythms of his life and work, used to come into the house, then go, and then return again.[7]

I think it is not the economic man, the scientific man, the political man, or the man as artist, but the fundamental religious man who thus journeyed far to a shrine in search of the origin of his life, trying by the power of an astonishing memory to remember God; and I think that the use of one word here instead of another reveals with heartbreaking profundity the pathetic man of our time; the

[7] *The Hills Beyond,* pp. 37–38.

word is "Absence." I cannot doubt that Wolfe knew what word he
was using, what it meant, its full measure of pathos, and that he
was conscious of the other word, replete with tragedy and healing,
that might have been used if he had been able to find it true: the
word is "Presence." Perhaps the Mother had left him to go spend a
long afternoon at the Fair, and the terrible shock of Absence had
broken in upon the child's soul; and until he conquered the wound
of Absence (which may be the wound of birth itself) he could
never go home again into the Father's Presence.

Wolfe had a good grip on the words of personal anguish; he
would rise from his couch and speak in his troubled voice of the
pain of writing, of how his heart was being cut out, of the grievous
toil in the face of bitter sneers; and I was reminded of King David,
the Psalmist, an eloquent howler in tribulation: "I am poured out
like water, and all my bones are out of joint; my heart is like wax;
it is melted in the midst of my bowels." But I did not think it was
the effort of writing, the demands of his editor, the yelp of critics,
or the myopia of his readers that gave him so great pain. This white
blaze of Absence, at the core of his memory, would grant nothing;
and everything—the uttermost atom of the universe—had to be
sought, remembered, devoured, to put some everlasting potency in
the place of this damnable Absence. In this way, surely, the pathetic mind of modern man is stricken. Wolfe's word of anguish is
more eloquent than mine:

All this hideous doubt, despair, and dark confusion of the soul a lonely
man must know, for he is united to no image save that which he creates
himself, he is bolstered by no other knowledge save that which he can
gather for himself with the vision of his own eyes and brain. He is
sustained and cheered by no party, he is given comfort by no creed,
he has no faith in him except his own. And often that faith deserts him,
leaving him shaken and filled with impotence. And then it seems to him
that his life has come to nothing, that he is ruined, lost, and broken past
redemption, and that morning—bright, shining morning, with its prom-

ise of new beginnings—will never come upon the earth again as it did once.[8]

I believe, to a benign and calm beholding, such huge effort to remember God was not hopeless, was not in vain, for shadowy behind the blaze of Absence, and held out of reach by the throes of fierce pride, was the immanent miraculous concept of God, waiting to be touched and brought present by the receptive humility of self-forgetfulness: when suffering exhausted the arrogance of memory and stilled the passionate pleading of self, God might be given in the end.

When we got out on the street, under the evening lights, I made a remark about a young woman we had both noticed, drinking near us at the bar. He said,

"A man remembers a lot of women, and one woman. And then you know it wasn't what you wanted; but part of it was what you had to have. I believe in life. I think every great writer has believed in life. By God, I believe in life!"

But with his heart aching for "the lost lane-end into heaven," not by all the power of his miraculous memory had he yet been able to remember God.

"Here in this House, this Absence—here am I."

We strode on toward the flash and resonant rumble of Broadway at the hour of theatre opening. We knew a place to go in the turmoil for food and further talk.

[8] *The Hills Beyond*, p. 189.

6. A PSYCHIC DISTURBANCE

I think *King Lear* is the most wonderful psychic disturbance in literature, and it should be experienced seven times in order to understand Wolfe. It should be experienced seven times in order to understand any man. But I would not stop there, for I think the *Agamemnon* trilogy of Aeschylus is the most wonderful resolution in literature of vast psychic disturbances; and I would take that seven times into my heart also. And the human psyche would then still remain beyond understanding.

Anyone who has read *Of Time and the River* knows that the neurotic splendor of Thomas Wolfe wrote large. His writing bangs on the exultant gongs of our fears and terrors, for he was, among other things, a master singer of our neurotic times; and I dare say that many a troubled reader harbors Wolfe's work to his or her bosom for this reason, that his books are fat with the eloquence of refuge and revenge and suffering magnified. Poets toil with these pregnant conflicts within the human psyche; they bear that fruit other than bread by which man lives. They bear the fruit of death, too.

Of Time and the River was a long way from being finished.

Wolfe had written hundreds of pages for the book; but on the middle summer day when he reached Newtown, in trouble, he had not yet written the opening of the book. That opening, "Orestes: Flight before Fury," was blocked on the threshold of creative consciousness by a psychic conflict.

He had been laboring on his book in the sullen heat of the city; he had lost his savor to weariness; what he needed was fresh air, relaxation and the salt wild spume of joy blowing on his heart; but he had gone into the country for the week-end in the company of five liberal young intellectuals, and the composite garment of their interweaving neuroses was upon him like the shirt of Nessus, holding him, as Hercules, "Foiled in the tangle of a viewless bond."

It was on a Sunday afternoon that he thus turned up in Newtown, sick with fear, and called me on the telephone.

"Hello, Bob?—Bob! I'm here—in Newtown—at a place called The Fountain Lunch."

I heard trouble in his voice. I was amazed to hear him speaking from Newtown, for only a couple of weeks before I had had a letter from him saying, in part:

Yes, I am in Brooklyn thinking a great deal about the hills and preparing to take a little excursion down to Baltimore and Gettysburg with Max Perkins, Friday . . . Your inquiry whether I am in Brooklyn or Hell at the present time somehow makes me think of General Sherman's statement that if he owned both Hell and the State of Texas he would give Texas away and go to Hell to live. It is steaming up again here and I think we are in for a spell of hot weather. I think I will be here most of the summer but may go away, probably to North Carolina, in the autumn. If you come to town call me up anyway . . .[9]

It would not have surprised me to have him telephone from Baltimore, Gettysburg, North Carolina, Brooklyn, Texas, or Hell—but Newtown!

[9] Unpublished letter, July 19, 1933.

"These people I am with," he was saying, "are on the way back to New York, and I told them I had promised to stop off at your place, and made them detour through Newtown to leave me."

"You're sure welcome, Tom. I hope you can spend the night, too."

"That's what I told them. Is that all right? I can't ride another mile with them. I won't get back in their damned car again."

"I'll be over for you in my car in less than ten minutes. I'm glad you thought of me and called."

"Listen, Bob. They're parked out here in front of the church. They're going to hang around till they see you come for me. They think I'm lying."

"You probably thought so yourself. I'll be right over to make you an honest man."

He managed about a quarter of a chortle.

"Thanks. That's fine of you, Bob."

I could hear his voice improve somewhat, as if a phobia had relaxed its stranglehold on his throat and at least the lie by which he had hoped to escape from his tormentors was loosened from his gullet. As for my being fine about it, that's the way he felt. The way I felt, as I told Marguerite the good news, was that Tom Wolfe was a clear, direct, and trusting friend, and I was about to have the pleasure of welcoming him for the first time into my home. My wife would meet him, my children would meet him, he would eat at our table and see how we lived. These are good things between friends.

Matters between a man and himself in the craggy world of psychic disturbance are not so simple. I believe Tom was in agony, while I raised dust along the road into town, through the sunny summer air. I believe this now. Then, having but heard his voice and having not yet seen him, I thought he was merely at the mild level of disappointment, irritation, or boredom. I soon got a better knowledge of his trouble, and before the day was over I had guessed half of it. I could have guessed more, a couple of weeks later when I got a letter from him, written on yellow paper with pencil, the joyous frantic words stamping line by line across the page, each word easy to see, but many of them smote down with such passion as to be squashed out of easy reading form. I could have guessed the rest, many months later, when *Of Time and the River* was published and I could read its first eighty-six pages. But (as I expect to say more fully in a later chapter) I read *Of Time and the River, Paradise Lost,* and the plays of Aeschylus at one lying in the hospital, and thought then of other things than this Sunday pain. It is only now, in meditation, that I put all these fragments together to take measure of Wolfe's distress at that crisis of psychic storm.

He left the telephone, went out of the Fountain Lunch, walked past the A & P store, crossed a narrow dirt road, and took his sombre stand in front of the Congregational Church, under the full maple trees, beside the automobile full of those people. He would not get into their damned car again. In front of him was the flagpole, with the American flag high in the sun and wind, and the highway leading off down a steep hill toward New Haven and Hartford; he could see far off under a blue sky the hills beyond Lake Zoar; to his left the highway ran under elm and maple trees toward Danbury, and to his right toward Bridgeport under dark green and sun-sprinkled summer boughs. He did not know from which direction his succor would come for he did not know in which direction from town I lived; he had never seen my automobile and did not know what sort or color of car to watch for— moreover, I suspect, all automobiles were similar shiny beetles to him.

Meantime, as I put it together now on the evidence of that joyous letter then unwritten, which was to describe a huge spate of writing done after he left my place, the footfalls of fury were sounding in his deep mind; a vast psychic disturbance was trying to surge up to the level of creative consciousness; "Orestes: Flight before Fury" was on the threshold; and now this phobia had set up a psychic block and enslaved his might in petty bonds. This was sufficient inner strangulation for one mortal on a Sunday afternoon in summertime. It would bring beads of sweat out on a strong man's face. And yet, I suppose he was cold, too, the great wild vine root of his rampant heart being frozen tight in the bitter ground of a psychogenic chill.

I drove along through the redolent and splendid warmth of August; the warm, gentle, and wandering wind was laden with rich smells of ripeness gathered from the swamps, the woods, the orchards, and the fields; even the stones of New England seem mellow in the August hours of crowning ripeness.

I saw him from a distance. He was standing beside a cherry red sedan which was parked in front of the white church. His bulging briefcase was on the ground, leaning against one of his legs. He wore a brown suit, stretched to his living proportions, and a darker brown felt hat, which had been mauled and yanked in use until it now had the good, manly qualities of an old hat. He was considerably taller than the high 1932 automobile. This being the first time I had approached him in the open air from a distance, I got a vivid impression of what a massive work of nature his torso was. Some tall men are mostly legs; but Wolfe had hugeness in the body.

The man Wolfe, like Saturn, had seven rings of splendor round about him. Saturn was also fallen upon evil times, as Keats well knew. Wolfe was not sitting and was not grey-haired, "quiet as a stone," but standing bowed and sombre and dark-haired, under the maple trees in front of the Congregational Church.

> Forest on forest hung about his head
> Like cloud on cloud. . . .
> While his bow'd head seemed list'ning to the Earth,

His ancient Mother, for some comfort yet . . .
. . ."I am gone
Away from my own bosom: I have left
My strong identity, my real self
Somewhere . . ."

It was a phobia of considerable power, bred in his realms of vast imaginings, that had him in clutch.

I swung around the flagpole and stopped the car so that he stood between my blue car and the cherry red one. He had recognized me as I made the turn, and his great figure changed from an attitude of sombre and sulky stiffness to a kind of prancing, the kind I have seen a Percheron do on the icy streets of Omaha when, after getting up from a fall, he stands stiff while fright passes, then stirs throughout his body with renewed courage to lay into the collar and pull again.

From the red sedan, the faces of young men and women watched me come to a stop; their combined glances were as a stroke of dank cynicism, that hostile and unholy "O, yeah? So What?" of the bewildered American soul.

Wolfe knocked over his bulging and battered briefcase, striding nearer and stretching out his hand as I got out of my automobile.

"Hello, Bob!" he said with a kind of explosive force, and shook my hand firm and hard.

He had by this time given his necktie an awful twisting, tugging, and side-hauling, as if that poor limp green rag were the Strangler at his throat. He led me over to meet those people in the cherry dark shining car.

"I want you to meet my friend, Bob Raynolds."

I shook hands through windows and across bodies.

There was not a happy face among the five. I suppose by this time they were to Tom a carload of incarnate neuroses, and you might as well ride with a mess of tigers. To me, not involved in

their doings, they looked like a carload of commonplace intellectuals, nervous, beset, tormented young people, who made the noise
of liberalism with undue ferocity because they have allowed their
own inward lives to be ruled by tyrannous fears. And there was
about them as a group something prismatic, like a rainbow: the
red woman, the purple woman, and the brown woman, the blue
man and the green man; the blue man was the driver and the red
woman sat next to him, while the green man sat in the back seat
between the brown woman and the purple woman. This sounds
fantastic, but I find it easier to give them colors than names. And it
seemed to me that there was not a yielder of solace among them.
Chaucer, that amiable man of morning clarity, speaks "of mirth
and solace," and in his gentle poem so well renders both to the
world as to be good for us still after these hundreds of years. It is
pathetic to be so tethered and whipped continually by your anxieties that you have never the serenity in your soul to yield solace
to a friend or an enemy or to a stranger. These five yielded each an
intense color of sharp distress.

"Thank you for bringing Tom," I said to them. "If you're going
to New York, my place will be only half a mile out of the way. Why
don't you follow behind me and stop off for a glass of beer? I've got
plenty on ice."

There was a darting of colors back and forth from face to face,
until the blue man smiled. He was the least secretive soul of the
lot, and when seen separately, in a good light, had the lovely traces
of sorrow behind his successful façade.

"Thanks, Raynolds," he said. "We can't stop long, but a cold
beer would be good at this point."

There was something in the way he said this that sounded like,
"Damn you, Tom, for pulling a fast one! But you haven't got away
from us yet."

I swept a last glance over them before Tom and I turned to my car. Tom, still awkward with tension, picked up his briefcase and got in, bumping his head and knocking his hat awry. As we started off, he was staring straight ahead down the road, the champ of his jaws flexing his cheeks, as if he were chewing on grim thoughts. Of course I had by now seen enough to realize it would be a strain to spend a long time in that complex society of maladjusted people; but the result they had produced in Wolfe seemed disproportionate to the cause. Had they done something, said something, combined against him in some way? What was choking him? Wolfe, to be sure, never waited for the waggling of tongues: he heard the loud discourse of a man's being on sight, and those five were a roaring picture. When I swung around the first turn the change of direction broke the fixity of Tom's stare.

"Did you ever hate anybody so much," he asked "that you couldn't go to the bathroom in their house?"

I could see in my mirror the red sedan following us, turning now off the highway onto the dirt road.

"Since when?"

"I sneaked out of their house last night, but not since."

"I'll take the bumps easy. They're following right behind us, so there's no use to stop by that clump of woods ahead. But I tell you what—I've got a good, old-fashioned outhouse beside the white barn. You beat it for that as soon as I stop the car, and I'll keep them talking about the dog when they get out of theirs. I can count on Storm to jump all over them; he's a fine dog."

Tom sighed and nearly smiled. Relief was in sight. Well, he said, those people weren't so bad, maybe, after all. Not one by one; it was when you took them all together. He told me something about them. The dark-haired man, driving the car, was in the money end of writing—publicity and advertising, twenty-five thousand dollars a year, and more in prospect; his wife was insufficient to quell his anxieties, and he had given her a trip to

Mexico for the summer while he rented a house up near Washington, Connecticut, for week-end parties. His girl of the week (the red woman) wrote stories and serials for women's magazines. She had been married twice and psychoanalyzed once, and she wore her clothes tight around her hips, her belly, and her breasts, as if swathing strange secrets inside her wrappings. The little blond (green) man in the back seat was in one of the new publishing houses. He suffered from money-misery, sick with coveting. His friend was the purple woman, who had a business of her own. The brown woman had been company for Tom. She was somebody's secretary down around Wall Street, and what she liked best of all was to eat.

"They came to my place Friday afternoon," Tom said, "all ready to leave, and I needed a rest and change. That's how I got into it."

He didn't have anything against them, one by one; but the panorama they had presented to his senses, of frustration, inhibition, libertinism, secretive greeds and foibles, had dragged him down, as if he had fallen into the hands of a gang of spiritual thugs; and in subtle ways they had ganged up on him, for, among the lot he alone had made of his life a spiritual struggle for great aims, and they had left their early aims by the way in sloth, fear, and lonely hurt, so that as a group, unconsciously, they were profoundly hostile to a man of Wolfe's large aims and true accomplishments. They wanted to whittle him down to their size. Simply, they wanted to cut his heart out. But hard as it may have been to endure this week-end with them, I doubt not that it increased his insight for writing, as he so often did, about the lost and ruined.

We reached a rise, and I nodded ahead toward a wonderful New England picture half a mile away. "There, Tom! You can see the place." The sunlight was on it clear and still: the white barn and the grey barn and the white plain house between, sheltered under the luminous green-gold domes of palpitant maple trees, and the aged dark-limbed apple orchard behind, and the stone-fenced earthy spread of pasture fields all around, to the edge of woods.

He looked straight at my place and saw it well, the way he was able to see a space of summer sunlight and a moment of time and a work of man once and for all and forever. And I suppose, when he called up the picture later in memory, the refractions of his profound solipsism would cast over it a sorrowful haunting and desolate light.

I turned into my driveway and stopped the car. The red sedan went past and rolled two wheels up onto the lawn under the maple trees. Tom sprang from my car and long-legged it toward the outhouse; that was, so to speak, my first real sight of Wolfe in the country, skedaddling around the corner of the barn, under the boughs of an old apple tree with yellow apples on it, toward the easy door of a homey outhouse. Meantime Storm, our Labrador Retriever, was prancing around the red sedan, eager to paw and lick and generally knock about with good cheer the arriving guests.

Storm was a noble black dog of great proportions, the most regal creature round about our place. (Though Storm has died now, I can spot his traces, to the third generation, in new dogs lolloping about the roads and farms: he had a good, unkenneled life, with our house as his headquarters. Wolfe also honored him doubtfully with a curious transmutation, for a massive black killer dog by the name of Storm turns up in one of Wolfe's later books.) The astonishment of seeing so bounding, great, and amiable a dog released the five people in the red sedan from the intricate bonds which had bound them there; they were able to get out, stand on their own feet, look the place over, play with Storm, ask all about him, brush off the dust, shake their bodies, and come around to the stone terrace in back of the house, where Tom joined us and Marguerite met us. In fact, these five people now seemed utterly separated from each other as we sat on the terrace drinking beer. The purple woman, who had a bouncing bosom and slender legs and wore her clothes freely, was plucking about here and there for Marguerite's background. The money-misery lad was trying to figure out how many dollars a place like ours cost, and wondering how in hell I did it by writing (I didn't). The brown woman had run down into the orchard, to a tree I pointed out, and now had her lap full of apples from one of the early ripening trees. The blue man and the red woman sat divided by that air of watchful contempt and hatred that sets apart a man and a woman who, having met for sexual satiation, have now in broad daylight no common spiritual bond. By this time they all had toward Tom that superior polite air of injured forgivingness under which people take shelter when you have told them, by word or act, that they sicken your very flesh; they indulged in nose lifting, slant glancing, and word poisoning. However, at one moment, Tom and the blue man and I exchanged glances; and then the three of us knew how much each of us had backed and filled to mend a painful situation; and joining in a spontaneous impulse, we lifted our glasses and drank to fellowship, being now on a manly and honest basis with each other. Tom actually adjusted his tie to a neater knot, as if the phobia were losing its hold on him.

But Wolfe was not talking. He would laugh "Ho! Ho!" or say "Ha!" or utter a sentence of three words, such as "this is nice," or one of four words, such as "Thank you, Mrs. Raynolds." Below the stone terrace Marguerite had laid out a semicircular garden, had poked her hands in the earth, and now the phlox and other August flowers were in bloom and fragrance. At the farthest point from the terrace, a path broke through this semicircle, and I had mowed it for about forty yards down into the orchard. The afternoon sunlight was on all of us and on our glasses of beer. Nevertheless, Wolfe was not talking. There was only one other occasion when I was with him in a group of as many as eight people, and that time he talked with simplicity and freedom; therefore I do not think he was a man who became tongue-tied when in the company of more than two or three, but rather that now the psychic block was still operant. At least, if it were passing, he was in that pallid state of inner exhaustion in which a man feels erased and has nothing to say. The purple woman slid her eyes over him presumptuously, as if to say, "So this is all there is left of the great man? Humph!" And this brought a sparkle of fury to Tom's eye, which was a good sign of his returning vigor, and scared her so much that she dropped her glass on the terrace and broke it and splashed beer suds on her bare legs.

When all this company arrived, Polly and the three children—David, Ann, and Barbara—had been down in the sand pit engaged in major operations beyond parental description. Polly was the young girl we employed to look after the children, and Polly employed the children to get into our midst. I had seen her rise up out of the sand pit, away off down in the sunlit field; I knew it would not be long before she thought up something for the children to ask us. And now they bore down on us. The children were in sunsuits. Barbara had on a straw hat, and being not yet much of a walker, clung to one of Polly's hands to be dragged along. Ann wore a red beret which she had loved for two years—all during the second half of her life to that time; it was cocked on one side of her head. David had no hat; his face was flushed and spangled with sweat and glee—evidently he had been doing the master shovel work. When they reached the edge of the terrace, the children came on, in their lovely splotches of dirt, to Marguerite's chair, and Polly, with direct and simple curiosity, stood with her hands on her hips looking us all over.

"Can we go to Donald's and play in the hay?"

This was the request, the new idea Polly had sold them, in order to get herself a good look at what was going on.

"Ask Cuckoo what he thinks," Marguerite said.

The three of them trotted over to me and asked,

"Cuckoo, can we go to Donald's?"

Something had surprised the guests. Even Wolfe looked at me curiously. It was not only that we had children, which so many tormented moderns considered an invasion of their "creative" freedom, but we also seemed to enjoy having children about, as real people, instead of ridding ourselves of them to brood over unresolved horrors of society and of our own blasted childhood. And, to top it off, these children called their father "Cuckoo." Our guests may even have suspected me of celebrating the delightful reality and companionship of children in books I wrote, a thing almost no serious author since Tolstoy had dared to do. An exclusion of children, disgust with the family, a sterile eroticism, and increasing brutality were becoming hallmarks of modern writing; but I wrote no book without the joy of children in it. And Wolfe came to share our joy in our children; and they responded to his chortles of pleasure.

"Cuckoo! Can we go to Donald's!"

Marguerite, under normal circumstances, would have said "yes" or "no" herself. But the night before we had been awakened by strange snortings and ground-beatings outside our window, and there in the moonlight, on the loose, was the lusty young bull from our neighbor's farm (Donald was the neighbor boy). This young bull had pawed around the grapevine; then he rolliked down the road toward the sand pit and the schoolhouse (where I wrote books), and knocked over a young pine tree Marguerite had planted for me in front of the school house; next he broke through a gate and got up into one of our pasture lots, where he smelled the recent presence of cows. Another neighbor rents our pasture, and his cows were in their barn for the night; but the young bull was furious to smell them and not see them. He bellowed and banged the earth with his front feet. We telephoned Donald's father, who came with a rope with a snap on one end, snapped it into the ring in the young bull's nose, and led the animal gently home beneath stars.

"You can go," I told the children, "if you'll be careful about the bull." And I called across the heads of our guests to Polly, "Make sure the bull is either tied to his stake or shut in the barnyard, before you let the children go too near him." Polly stood there in careless plumpness and broad-bottomed ease, staring with youthful pleasure at the whole group. Polly had lots of brothers and sisters and liked looking at lots of people. A slight widening of her blue eyes acknowledged that she had heard me.

Barbara had gone back to take hold of Marguerite's knee, in that kind of standing-leaning-swaying posture that is normal in a two-year-old. The other two children, with suitable looks at the company, went off with Polly, who looked back at all of us a last time over her shoulder. Barbara preferred to stay. As Tom was sitting in the chair next to Marguerite's, Barbara reached out to pat his knee and pat his hand, still clinging with her other arm to Marguerite's knee. Barbara likes men: men like Barbara.

"What adorable children," the red woman said, with a shudder.

I got the impression that those five were knitting into a group again, that they felt out of their depth in such a prosaic setting; for here were two people who had been married to each other for six or seven years, who had three children, who lived in a fixed place, and who seemed to like it (it's full thirty years now, and still the same place, and eleven grandchildren now included); so much domestic normalcy was shocking to the emancipated, and surely left nothing to talk about. Without any one of them saying the word, they all rose to go.

"I certainly enjoyed those apples, Mr. Raynolds," the brown woman said. "What is it the children call you?"

"Cuckoo."

"I thought that's what they were saying."

"I called my father 'Sir!' " said the green man with (I thought) remarkable bitterness.

Each of the women kissed Tom goodbye, and I could tell by his reluctant stooping to their lips that he did not like it. When Erasmus first came to England, he was delighted to find it a custom there (in those days) for the young ladies to greet a famous stranger with kisses; thus he was joyously met in Thomas More's good house by Thomas More's fine daughters; and several centuries later Wolfe enjoyed this same custom in Denmark (so he told me) even as Erasmus had in England. But today those young women on the terrace were secretive and greedy instead of open, spontaneous, and happy, their avid lips seeking rather to brand him than to please him at parting; and I think that is why he recoiled from their kisses.

At last the red sedan dusted off down the road. Tom had the snorting look of a curly-browed bull calf that has just broken loose from the rope, gives a wild stare at the branding irons in the fire, and then hightails it off into the sagebrush. I began to laugh.

"That gang of spiritual dogie rustlers just about had you hog-tied, cut, and branded, Tom."

"Ha!" he snorted, looking at me and looking at Marguerite and looking way down at Barbara, and really smiling for the first time, but troubled still. "I never thought I was a prude," he went on, "but when three men and three women come to Connecticut for the weekend, do they have to swim in the pond naked without any clothes on?"

This chapter has no dramatic conclusion, but only the truce of twilight and evening's sweet settlement round about us in the

orchard. But I have raised a question concerning the inner motions of Wolfe's creative force. I have made this speculation: that
Tom, tired and run-down from hard work in the hot city, had come
to the country in a hypersensitive state, and some profound anxiety
(perhaps originating in his childhood, who knows?) had been
touched off by something, anything, in the complex contact with
those people; then, at the same time (perhaps born of old anxiety, too), there was rising in his creative mind the tremendous
psychic storm of "Orestes: Flight before Fury"; and the phobia
collided with the creative urge, producing a psychic paralysis so
strong as temporarily to impair even natural functions. We think
it not strange if an embolism in the brain paralyzes the arm or
tongue of a man; there are embolisms in the realms of imagination
and emotions, too; and Wolfe lived an exceedingly strenuous life
in the realms of imagination and emotion. As some persons de-
velop high blood pressure, so I think Wolfe in his way of work
(like Balzac) had developed about as high a psychic pressure as
the fibre of a man could long withstand; it was enormously pro-
ductive, and dangerous. Death indeed, though four or five years
yet away, was already on the march in the vast environs of his
forfeit life.

Evening fell about us, redolent, sweet and still, as we sat on the
terrace, Tom and Marguerite and I; the moon was up, the stars
came out, and lovely fireflies danced in the ambient dusk of the
nocturnal orchard. I could tell from the easy splendor of his
mellow voice that Tom had come back to his own bosom, his
strong identity, his real self. And perhaps already the apprehension of clear purpose had begun to make his heart beat strong
again. To create again would be natural, functional.

We three talked together of books, of folk, and of the earth;
summer night and the smell of earth were about us; Storm passed
sometimes down among the apple trees in the silent noble motion

of a solitary world creature, then came to snuffle round our knees, patiently informing us about life out there on the spread of ground.

In the peace of the night and our comfort of communion, Tom told us, with childlike sadness, that he often dreamed he was walking on the Aegean shore and that Medusa rose up before him and came toward him in her graceful, self-possessed step; a mistress of delight had become a Medusa of nightmare; by some bewildering estrangement of soul, a love had become a horror.

Then, in the shelter of our home, he broke the sorrow of that haunting with a half-humorous, half-poignant plea, "Margaret [he never called her Marguerite], I wish you would find me a nice girl to marry."

For a lone man comes back to his room in a building, dreading the waste silence of twilight on the walls.

When the bell-clear, silver-clear, half-moon set behind the clear ridge of our westward barn, we went into the shelter of the house for the resting of night.

His eyes sparkled the next morning; he ate breakfast with gusto in the midst of our little and big pancake eaters; I took him to the train in Bethel, and he went rampant back to the city, the psychic block thawed out.

Some days later I got that remarkable, joyous letter, postmarked August 29, 1933; I think about half of it ought to be quoted here, for it points specifically to the mood in which he wrote the opening of *Of Time and the River:*

Dear Bob:
I haven't had my typist here in a week—hence my lazy failure in writing you. It was so nice being out there at your place—I think the place is magnificent and have never seen a finer family and such affectionate children. Can I come again and stay *two* days—and when can I come? If I come can we have some more hot cakes—they seemed

the best I'd ever eaten. I am doing a very exciting piece of writing—at least it's exciting to me—so much so that I'm in a delirious mental state and a terrible physical condition—a sort of cross between delirium tremens and Olympian calm. Sometimes when I'm working at it I think it's going to be so good that I almost cry about it, but when I'm not working at it I curse God, men and everything. I'm calling my piece which like everything else is a section of the library *The Image Of Fury In The Artist's Youth*—is this a good or lousy title? I just slapped it down, so it can be changed, and thought of *In The Artist's Youth* as a subtitle and not really essential to it. Anyway, it's about Fury, not especially artist's fury, but the kind of fury young men have, probably more in this country than anywhere on earth—the [word illegible], exulting desire to eat and drink the earth, yelling into the wind on lonely roads, etc.—and it starts in just about the most furious way it can—on a train smashing Northwards across the state of Virginia at night, with three drunken youths—as drunk with the exultant fact and fury of going to the city for the first time, out to conquer the world, do everything, see all, etc—as with corn liquor they keep passing from bed to bed. . . . This is the first time I've told anyone about anything I'm writing in years. That itself is a youthful thing to do. . . . Don't tell on me. The train part is only one small part. I hope to see you soon. Love to all.

Tom Wolfe[10]

To those who are subtle interpreters of character, I wish to report the last remark Tom made, in our hallway, before I took him to his train. He was saying goodbye to Marguerite and thanking her for her hospitality. He called her "Mrs. Raynolds," and she said, "Call me 'Marguerite'." He looked embarassed a moment, then he said,

"Thank you, Margaret. I don't know why I called you Missus. I don't even call my own mother Missus."

In the many years since, I have not yet figured that one out.

[10] *Letters of Thomas Wolfe*, pp. 382–383.

7. MOUNTAIN JOURNEY

Breakfast and Departure

Marguerite and I puzzled a long time over some of the words in that excited letter, before we finally gave them up as illegible. They were in what Wolfe called his "Chinese script." We gave them another try upside down and in a better light. And finally we left four or five words unsolved. But it was clear that he wanted to come again, he wanted to say two nights, and he wanted some more hot cakes. I wrote, asking him to come.

I went over to Bethel to meet the train. As it slowed down, I saw through the car windows the shoulders and faces of people walking toward the vestibule to get off. I saw his figure overtopping the heads of the other travellers, but his head and face were cut off from my sight in the upper regions of the car. Then the train stopped and I saw him in the shadow of the vestibule, and I thought it was this shadow that gave his face a sick hue. He was traveling light, with the clothes on his back and the brown brief case bulging nearly round. (I must say, now that I mention this briefcase again, that it was not diplomat shiny or lawyer fancy or executive trim; Tom's briefcase, of a kind of worn and scuffed cholocate brown, reminded me more of the well-used and homey leather of a saddlebag in cow country; he carried it all for use and none for show.) He was too big to "emerge" or "step down" from the vestibule; he came down onto the platform like an avalanche of life, and stood there in clear light, shaking my hand.

It had not been only the shadow of the vestibule giving pallor to his face. It was not as firm and full and ruddy a round as usual; his cheeks sagged and he was grey. *Of Time and the River* was taking its toll. It was only two weeks since he had written: "I'm in a delirious mental state and a terrible physical condition."

On the platform people I knew gave startled glances. They were used to my being tall, but not to seeing me with a man four inches taller still.

We folded into my car and drove toward Newtown. Presently we heard the train whistle, off on its way from Bethel to Danbury. That train was pulled by an electric engine, and the whistle—but Wolfe noticed it too.

"That whistle doesn't sound train-size," he said "It isn't like the wonderful whistle of steam engines that you heard haunting the valleys and mountains when you were a boy."

"Once in a while, at night," I told him, "I can hear a steam engine whistle on another line, a freight line, about three miles from my house, and all at once I remember the great plains of the West that sweep out, under the moon, from the mountains, and a lonely train in a great space between far towns."

"And it whistles," Tom added with glee, "as it strokes down upon and across Main Street of a little town asleep—and a boy stirs in his bed with dreams of the City."

He was certainly no longer in a delirious mental state. His voice was gentle and tired, and his mind seemed calm as with exhaustion. That strenuous spate of writing, the heart of "Orestes: Flight be-

Oil painting by Robert Raynolds

Early spring in the haunting depth of the Great Smoky Mountains,
where Thomas Wolfe was born.

"Mountains were our cradle; and we loved the earth, our home."

Thomas Wolfe

At about the time of their first meeting—

"We both knew the toil and joy of writing novels, and we

Robert Raynolds

rought to each other the comfort and laughter of being friends."

Photograph by brother, Fred Wolfe
Courtesy of Estate of Thomas Wolfe

Thomas Wolfe in the doorway of his sister's home in
Asheville, within a year of his death.

"We were small-town boys and learned ou

Photograph by son, David Raynolds

Robert Raynolds in front of the house where he was
born, "The Old Palace," Santa Fe, a few days before the
death of Thomas Wolfe.

lives in the midst of ordinary people."

Thomas Wolfe

After years of writing—

"We had devoted our lives to

Robert Raynolds

saying the word of our manhood."

Watercolor by Robert Raynolds

Early autumn in the Sangre de Cristo Mountains where they endorse their majesty on the sky of New Mexico—and where Robert Raynolds was born.

"Mountains were our cradle; and we loved the earth, our home."

fore Fury," had evidently dissolved various psychic tensions, but it
had also burned up a store of physical vigor. He moved his hands
like great weights and did not bother to muss his hair. The man
was a few weeks from his thirty-third birthday, and a few days less
than five years from his death. Despite the grey in his cheeks, the
putty pallor around his eyes, and the profound tiredness of his
mouth, which were like the tentative searchings of death for un-
shakable footing, I was impressed by the immensity of life in him.
There is a sense of life in a great ship free upon the water that stirs
me; and beholding Wolfe always gave me an analogous joy.

He relaxed and spoke of his special reason for coming this time
—a vacation journey together into Vermont, that he had asked me
to plan for us.

"I went to Montreal over Labor Day with Fritz and Cornie
Dashiell," he said, "but it was a rush, they didn't have time to stop
off, and I want to go back to Vermont. I want to see the whole state
of Vermont."

"We'll have a good trip. I've got the time, and here's the automobile. My back is in suitably bad shape just now, so that a hundred or a hundred and fifty miles is as much as I want to drive in
a day. That will slow us down into taking our time."

"I wish I could help, but I'd wreck us if I tried to drive—They
have those beautiful green meadows up there."

It made him happy to see our house again in sunset light. He
was smiling when he greeted Marguerite (calling her "Margaret,"
which became fixed in his mind as her name) and he chortled at
the gravity with which David, the watchfulness with which Ann,
and the boldness with which Barbara greeted him. We talked until
supper was ready, but he did not get up from his chair to pace back
and forth; and after supper, feeling more at home with us, he lay at
great length on our dark green couch (which emphasized the pallor rather than the red of his face) and talked from there.

Marguerite and Tom were better talkers than I. Sometimes I made a comment, but mostly they talked, and got on famously. Listening to Tom was like listening to fragments of a wonderful narrative poem; and Marguerite speaks lyric poetry, as blithely unconscious of the radiance of her speech as M. Jordain was unconscious of speaking prose.

Having praised life until midnight, we got something to eat from the icebox, then went to bed.

In the morning the three little children sat at a little table in the dining room, and we three grown ones sat at the big table. Hot cakes came in rapidly from the kitchen. Conditions were evidently just right for contact to be made between the two tables. These children of ours had a remarkable somewhat that I have noticed in other gamins of field, street, and fireside; that is, they carried about with them ever abundant loads of childness—

> And with his varying childness cures in me
> Thoughts that would thick my blood. . . .

—and spilled this wonderful commodity round about them at every motion, word, glance, or feather breath of sleep. At first there was gossip and glancing among them while we ate in sober earnest, then giggles, then little accidents; and when I tried to calm them down by flicking a spoonful of water at them, the contact was established between the two tables, and the rest of the meal was a merry uproar, with the big table and the little table both involved. Finally a syrup-soaked tidbit of hot cake plopped against the wallpaper. I don't know the criminal; but all five of them, Marguerite, Tom, David, Ann, and Barbara, looked at me and agreed,

"Cuckoo started it!"

Thus condemned, I sponged at the spot with a rag and water, but it did no good; the spot remained there for years, soon flanked by others, until finally (when the children began to eat at the big table) we had the room repapered.

Mid-morning found us assembled on the front lawn, under and between the two great maple trees, with Storm furled on the green-bladed grass watching us. The car was ready, loaded with my suitcase, Tom's briefcase, a couple of robes and extra coats for the cool mountains of Vermont.

"You have a beautiful day for starting out," Marguerite said.

"Wait!" I exclaimed. "I have to get the guide-books!"

Tom looked at me in surprise. Was there a Baedeker to Vermont?

I seldom travel without guidebooks in which are explained the hazards of the journey and in which are puissant recipes for the necessities of life and perfected incantations against the fury of circumstance. I went back into the house and carefully brought to the car for this journey three of my best guidebooks to the world: Shakespeare, bound in roast-beef red, Aeschylus in pea-porridge green, and Montaigne in wine-grape blue. Tom looked at them, smacked his lips, and said, "Ha!"

Wolfe was sure a great talker.

As Tom took Marguerite's hand and bowed in courtesy and smiled and said goodbye there under the two great maples in morning light and leafy green flicker, I could still notice the grey ravage of his ambition and labor in the city; it was a deathly stain under the shape of his face, under the skin, under the pigmentation, that tightening of nerves and twitch of mouth that comes after the consumptive fires of creation have burned along the spine and through the brain.

By now Marguerite had the Shakespeare open, and was saying, "Don't forget Antony and Cleopatra."

And she chanced upon a passage and read:

> " 'Give me mine angle; we'll to the river: there,
> My music playing far off, I will betray
> Tawny-finn'd fishes; my bended hook shall pierce

Their slimy jaws, and, as I draw them up,
I'll think them every one an Antony,
And say, "Ah ha! You're caught".' "

To which I replied out of Aeschylus:
" 'Strife is the last of gods to end her tale' " and " 'Cast not the
seed of reckless words to crop the land with woe'."
And Tom concluded with the wine of Montaigne:
" 'Presumption is our naturall and originall infirmitie. Of all
creatures man is the most miserable and fraile, and therewithall
the proudest and disdainfullest. Who perceiveth and seeth himself placed here, amidst the filth and mire of the world, fast tied
and nailed to the worst, most senseless, and drooping part of the
world, in the vilest corner of the house, and farthest from heaven's
coape, with those creatures that are the worst of three conditions;
and yet dareth imaginarily place himself above the circle of the
moon, and reduce heaven under his feet'."
We tossed the guidebooks into the back seat, and set forth, joyously, to reduce the mountainous state of Vermont under our feet.

The House at Pownal Center

With our staunch forebears and masters of the word of man—
Aeschylus, Shakespeare, and Montaigne—scattered and visible in
the back seat, Tom began business with road maps, while I had
business driving.

I knew the road to Vermont all right, but Tom was studying
maps of Connecticut and Massachusetts while we drove northward along the Housatonic River. He was looking for mountains.
There was nothing exquisite about his handling of a road map. He
opened one wide, slapped out creases, made new ones where con-
venient, his only care being not to flap it in the driver's line of
vision. He put his finger on places, and roved over one state and

another with quick glances, not forgetting to look up—consume—population and mileage figures. I think he had good eyesight, for he never tried to adjust the distance between his eyes and the map, and he didn't strain or squint to see better.

"Nothing you could call a mountain, before Greylock," he announced. "Three thousand three hundred and five feet. That's pretty good." That was reading small print in a moving car.

"These crowded hills open out around Falls Village, and you can see ten or twenty miles, which is space for a breath," I told him.

He studied the map again.

"They have a Mount Everett here, over by Sheffield, but they don't give any altitude for it, so I guess it's not much."

"There are a couple more, mild not rugged, between Great Barrington and Hillsdale. I spent a summer in those parts once, while I was still in college, on account of love. I used to look over the tops for the real range beyond, hankering for the lift of Santa Fe or Denver."

"I'm going to see the Rocky Mountains."

"They rise up and they stretch out."

"This is a great country. There is no country like it. I used to lie in some hotel room in Europe and remember the spaces and names of America, and the feel and smell of our things."

We got our view of Greylock as we approached, passed, and looked back. Finally we got out of the car, stood on the road, and took a long look, until we considered Greylock devoured, although it was in Massachusetts instead of in Vermont.

To head for the mountains with a brother was an old, familiar, and happy pattern of my early life.

I now had the fine feeling that Tom and I travelled as friends and brothers toward the mountains of Vermont. It was the first time in nearly fifteen years that I had gone a journey not alone or man-and-woman style, but with a brother man; and I suspect the comfort of this brotherly mood had also become rare for Wolfe, and that now he enjoyed it, for the first friends in each of our lives had been older brothers.

Here at the heart of our story I set apart this theme and chord of our companionship. Tom's brother Ben and my brother Dick, our childhood companions of trust in mountain places, had been for each of us the first profound and sheltering companion who in mutual love helped us learn to live, and our response of trust and love helped them live. Each of us long ago in childhood had learned what it is to be a brother and to love a brother. Now Tom and I, on our first mountain day together, began to know that brotherhood as man to man was the profoundest chord of love and life that bound us together in friendship. A sonnet of long ago to my brother Dick sounds this deep chord and music of brotherhood:

> We rode between two mountains toward the sky
> And felt the western wind upon our faces;
> We slept where sounding waters swirled by
> Or built our evening fire in silent places;
> We shared the morning cliff and noon-weighed plain,
> Smelt sand and grass and windy forest pine,
> Or crossed a stream we never crossed again,
> Or watched the heavy heron's twilight line
> Of flight above a marsh; and sometimes spoke,
> And sometimes sped our meaning with our eyes,
> And often with a gesture could evoke
> Our harmony of venture and surmise:
>   We have this treasure until final rest,
>   That we were friends and brothers in the West.

So now Tom and I came into our brotherhood, happy and trustful together, breathing mountain air in mountain places; and we became more deeply, until Tom died, companion brother men in meeting, in pleasure, in converse, in silence, in trust; we became compassionate human brothers together in the deep ranges of intuition and insight, and in helping one another live.

Beyond Williamstown I nosed the car up the long hill into the air and upland terrain of Vermont. There was a farmhouse in wide sunlight on the open shoulder of the hill, and on the road a sign: "Grandview Farm—Overnight Guests."

"This looks like a good place to wake up in the morning," I said.

Tom had been looking around at the hills and down into the deep valley. At the edge of the highway, about forty yards apart, stood a man and a woman, each before an easel, painting the grand view.

"You're sure it's Vermont?" Tom asked.

"By a good four or five miles."

"It looks good to me."

The woman who managed the farmhouse looked up at us and said she had a room but that the beds were ordinary length.

"We're used to that."

"I guess you have to be."

She showed us a room under the eaves, with two white iron beds and a double window overlooking the barnyard. We could stand up in the middle of the room, between the beds, but we had to duck to get through the doorway.

"You can get supper in Bennington, but I'll give you breakfast."

We followed her downstairs to sign the guest book. That guest book should have trembled at our approach.

The hero of *Look Homeward, Angel*, in his college days, "would go to little towns he had never before visited. He would register at hotels as "Robert Herrick," "John Donne," "George Peele," "William Blake," and "John Milton" . . . " Now the boy had grown up, to sign his own poet-name in his own right.

Tom signed the book large: Thomas Wolfe—Brooklyn, and on

the next line I signed it large: Robert Raynolds—Newtown. I know what was in my vainglorious mind: "Here are a couple of famous fellows! Some later tourist will see our names together, and gape in wonder, and wish—oh, wish!—he had been there that same night!" I won't guess what was in Tom's mind, but his signature was even bolder than mine; and when I glanced rapidly at a shelf of books there in the living room of the farm house, he was doing the same. But Wolfe and Raynolds were not among the titles.

We tossed Montaigne, Aeschylus, and Shakespeare onto the beds, and went out walking in sunlight upon the hill. When we reached a place where the view was wide open and we could look down on the farmhouse, Tom said,

"Look, Bob, your back's tired, I know. Would you mind if I climbed on up to the top?"

"Go ahead, Tom. I'll sit here smoking my pipe and looking around."

Upward was a ledge of rocks crowned with aspen trees and, for the mountain born, a sure sense of knoll and height above and beyond. I watched him stride off, up among the rocks and aspen trees. He was a proper sized man to be seen striding on hill shoulders and clambering ledge rock. He shouted and waved back to me from the ledge, in a flash of sunlight, then strode out of sight among the aspen trees.

He came prowling back inside an hour, a dark, majestic youth; the stain of the city was gone out of his face; and now he stood on the mountainside in the sun—very Man in his youth and pristine splendor. I do not mean caveman, long-armed, round-shouldered; or precivilized man as the romantic, Rousseau nonsense would have him; but rather man possessing that upright and radiant principle which has made some few men noble and many men less savage.

"What did you see, Tom?"

"It was farther than I thought to the top, and still there were higher places beyond. I could see Greylock, and down over Massachussetts, and mountains east and mountains north. It's like being in the mountains at home. That one across the deep valley there, that could be down home."

"There are places like this in Colorado, except you would see a stone peak above timberline beyond. It's so much green that hampers me."

"At home they're green, and may be a lot higher than here. And a haze in the air."

"This is good, though. Look at the quarry way over there, and that steam engine snorting in the valley."

"That train must be nearly two thousand feet below us. This is going to be a wonderful trip."

He stretched his arms and filled his lungs.

We drove in to Bennington for supper, came back to the farm, then took an evening stroll on the highway, through Pownal Center and back. Pownal Center was a village of few houses, and one of them right near the road is a little square frame house coated with fading orange paint. I've passed it many times in the years since, in auto and afoot. I wonder why it haunts me. Is it the color, the shape, the air of lonesome humble life about it? May be, somehow, it reminds me of an adobe house in the Southwest; a bit of the color of western earth standing exiled in New England green? I told Tom I always looked for that house when I came this way. There on the road, hands on his hips and cigaret at ease in his lips, he contemplated the house in the evening light. He seldom spoke with a cigaret in his mouth. He removed it before speaking.

"I see what you mean, Bob. It's dingy, it's run-down, it's poor. There is no other house just like it in all the world; and yet there is the simple and naked soul of shelter for man."

Good Smells at Morning

I woke up early in the morning.

I saw Tom, in trousers and undershirt, at the end of the room, looking out one of the windows. He had leaned his bare right arm on the top of the window frame, and was looking down through one of the top panes; his bare shoulders were against the eave, and his head was bent, much as if he were holding up the roof over that part of the house, while he looked intently at something beyond my vision. His expression was concentrated and intent, not dreamy; I might call it the intaking or harvesting expression, that sharply defined his face while he was gleaning from the world.

I straightened out in my bed, shoving my feet against the white iron at one end and my head against the white iron at the other, then pushing my feet between the bars and out the end. My covers were pulled askew. Across the narrow room the white iron bed Tom had slept on had been thoroughly mauled; the covers had been thrashed onto the floor, the pillow was jammed between the head of the bed and the wall, and the bottom sheet was pulled away from the mattress. The tools and appliances of comfort in this world are not built to the measure of oversize men. I toyed for a moment with the question of whether or not Wolfe felt his spirit hampered too in the confines of current opinion, where so many souls drowse snug. Then I was wide awake and realized the question was silly. As one of the three guidebooks pointed out: " . . . not in our stars, But in ourselves . . ."

The mild splendor of morning sunlight came in onto the floor and by refraction lit up Wolfe's strong young face. He had slept in his underwear but had put on his pants before going to the window; his sleeveless undershirt revealed the mass and power of his torso to store up deep fires and passions and knowings of the bowels of life, even as Tolstoy was built to like power; his great bare arms, rather than bulging with muscles, were smooth, as was natural in a man laboring to build a world with a pencil. I saw him take a deep breath.

"Good morning, Tom. How do you like the smell of manure?"

He looked around at me with that vivid alertness of an animal startled in solitude; then he accepted my intruding wakeful consciousness as friendly, and smiled welcome.

"It's one of the great, healthy smells of the world," he said.

"It ought to cure a man's soul of too much Brooklyn."

I got out of bed and went to look through the top of the other window. We stood there looking down into the barnyard, which was pockmarked by cattle spoors and mottled dank and rich with manure. Among the congeries of great red barns we saw the farmer loading manure into a wagon; russet chickens pecked about his sunlit legs, and one of the hired men was urging the herd of milk cows through a gate into the high hillside pasture. We could smell hay and fresh milk and moist earth, touched with rambling whiffs of morning mountainside breeze.

"There's silage, too; I can smell it fermenting."

"It's good to be alive, Bob."

"And good to know it."

"That's what all great writers keep saying, even when they seem bitter, like Swift. I know great writers loved every minute of their living, even the agony."

"Like Carlyle on a rampage—What's that creeping under the crack of our door, Tom?"

He looked toward the crack under the door. Nothing was visible, but he pursed his lips and sniffed with his active nostrils, then rolled his eyes to give me a shrewd sideglance.

"Bacon!" he pronounced.

"And coffee!"

Even authors have some moments in which their reactions are

normal. We responded to the odor of bacon and coffee with swift thought and sane action: we thought of breakfast, we washed, dressed, went downstairs into the farmhouse dining room; and there we found and (contrary to Freud's dicta that the goal of life is death) we joyously consumed, for present pleasure and to prolong life, milk, cereal, bacon, eggs, toast, marmalade, apple pie, and coffee, followed by more coffee.

Pine; Mountain; Stone

About an hour later, we stopped in Bennington for a bite to eat, just hot cakes, maple syrup, sausages, and coffee, to keep us alive, and some canteloupe to balance our diet.

Although Wolfe was a strong talker on subjects large, general, profound, and evocative of the deep emotions that make a work of art vibrant, he was reticent about himself in homely matters. If you asked him what he had been doing or how he had been feeling, the answer would be Burtonesque or Miltonic, giving an impression that his spirit had been beating about the bushes of chaos and old night. He more readily spoke of the latest news from the fringes of Hell than of the splinter in his finger. But in the Bennington restaurant he was at sufficient ease with me to volunteer some personal commonplace matter.

"I think it was ptomaine poisoning," he said. "Anyway, I was pouring out that piece about fury, and Brooklyn was hot, and my nerves were terrible. I couldn't hold anything on my stomach. I'm sick of the boiled and steamed food in restaurants, and I got so I'd turn away at the door when I smelled the stuff. This trip is just what I need; I'm getting back my strength. It's good to be able to eat again."

I had a spasm of hay fever on the road out of Bennington; I sneezed and snorted and my eyes began to flow copious tears.

Tom was concerned; he thought it might be painful. I reassured him that it was merely a nuisance, promising no danger at all, other than that, in a moment of sneezing blindness, I might drive us into a truck or a tree. This did not concern him. Not being a driver himself or habituated to personal ways of handling a car on the road, he had the innocent confidence with which one rides in a train or a bus. I drove awhile with one hand, a handkerchief in the other to mop my eyes and blow my nose. A swerve of the car, although on a clear stretch of highway with nothing coming, shocked me into prudence. I slowed down and, arriving at a likely spot, stopped.

We got out and took a walk along an old road running up into a mountainside stand of pine. It was undoubtedly a planting, for the trees stood apart, well grown, of somewhat equal height, and clear of underbrush. From behind us over our shoulders shafts of sunlight filtered down through the treetops to splash the trunks and the grassy road. It was still, cool, crystalline, and fragrant where we walked; Tom, without a hat, his dark hair curly, walked tall and free among the splendid trees, through shadow and sun. Not as he walked in the city, peering, watchful, ready to pounce on a perception, nor as he strode the mountainside pasture the day before, prodigal and exultant, but rather with a relaxed, a gentle, a lyric pace; and the sparkling liquor of his dark eyes and the ease of tensions around his mouth made it seem that he had, for the moment, no ache of inner strain. I really believe that for ten or twenty minutes, there in the pine woods, he forgot about his book. We sat a while on a log and gossiped; my spasm of hay fever passed, we looked up to see how the sky, showing in tiny patches through green breaks in the pine tops, was a deep, intense, and brilliant blue.

We resumed our journey northward. Tom spread a map on his knees, studied it, then kept wary lookout to right and left, lest any mountain exceed our grasp. If the map named a mountain and gave its altitude, he made sure we saw the fellow and reduced it under our feet, by a sort of swift mind's-eye mounting. He would check with me for our road locations.

"Shaftsbury. Arlington coming."

"We got the Dome, 2,754 feet, back at the farm last night. Those two across the valley were White Rock, 2,628, and Bald Mountain, 2,693. And there's another Bald we got while you were sneezing out of Bennington, 2,865, and before Bennington, The Elbow, 2,587, and Mt. Anthony, 2,345. The population of Bennington is over five thousand, according to the mark here. That must be Spruce to our left, 3,060, and Glastonbury back right, 3,764. We'll bag a lot of 3,000-footers from now on, and Equinox is nearly 4— yes, 3,816."

"A handsome mountain, too. They look bigger when they stand out alone, like Equinox."

"We'll get them all. Ha! This is good!"

Sometimes I didn't agree with him. I would stop the car, we would both study the map, then survey the hills west or the hills east. If need be, we got out on the road for a clear view. I didn't think we could see Stratton, on account of the foreground foot-hills; but he was sure that from a certain rise in the road he had nailed Stratton, and I let him have it, as it were by default, 3,859 feet. After taking Green (3,185) on our left and Bromley (3,260) on our right, we rested our eyes in the valley for a mile or two around East Dorset. I said I thought Sinclair Lewis had a place over in Dorset or South Dorset, on another road, and Tom told quite a long story about meeting Lewis in England and going places with him. I thought from the way he talked that he was working at his book again, and that what he was telling me would sooner or later be worked out in writing.

Then we came to the marble.

There must at one time have been an active quarry high on the abrupt hillside. Steep trackways came down to the road, and at the edge of the highway on our left was a railroad siding, the skeleton of steelwork for a loading trestle, and a jumble of massive blocks of white marble. The place was deserted, sunlit and still.

"My father got stone from Vermont. I think most of it came from near Barre. The granite. But I want to feel this marble."

We got out of the car and went among the great blocks of marble. He touched them with his fingers, rubbed them with his palms, slapped them, hit them with the cushion of his fist, put his nose close to smell their clean stone smell, stood off to size them up, commented on cracks and on blocks with no cracks visible, then clambered over several big ones. He moved and spoke with ecstasy. Finally, with glee on his face and glory in his eyes, he sat on the hugest block of all, as on a pedestal rough hewn from the mighty ribs of earth, and I took a photograph of him there in the sun. Thus he celebrated the memory of his father, and refreshed his soul.

Kitchen; College; and Shirt

We ate lunch in Rutland, then turned east. We stopped at a proper point on the road, got out of the car, and looked at the mountains.

"That's Killington for sure," he said. As he talked he loosened his brown necktie and whipped it off. I don't think he liked wearing neckties or wearing his collar buttoned. He wanted his breathing and his thinking to be free, and no bottleneck between them. "And the one to the left is Pico."

Gathering Pico Peak (3,967) and Killington Peak (4,241) to our affectionate bosoms, we drove up toward the sky and stopped in the pass. Here we again got out, to read signs on the Long Trail, one at each side of the road, telling the distances to huts and to mountains. Such a trail was not to be neglected. We walked along the trail, so that it could no longer be said that we had not trod that trail and reduced it under our feet utterly. Where we walked it was an easy trail, with only a few rough spots of rude, dark stone. Tom was ahead of me at the first of these, and I saw at once that when he got into rough going he knew he had hands as well as feet. He did not try to balance and step, balance and step, but used four members to clamber. He liked this jaunt in the redolent, murmurous woods. We walked south till we reached a shelter hut. We imagined how it would be to sleep there nights; we experienced the deep woods and the high ridge, saw autumn color in fern and leaf of the high forest, and took great breaths of mountain air. We could have walked on, over log and stone, between Pico and Little Pico, between Killington and Little Killington, on and on to the very nose of Greylock; therefore we considered it as good as done.

Enlarged by so much advenure we returned to the car and soon headed north along Route 100. There was that fine view, at the turn, of mountains among mountains ahead. There had already been frost in this world; yellow and pink were among the birches on the great slopes and dark patches of spruce and hemlock loomed more grand because of the coming color in the deciduous trees. The stray clouds were wind-puffed, sunlit, and gorgeous.

Down we went into valley deeps and soon began to see the gem green meadows of the central mountain valleys of Vermont. No other meadows that I have seen sparkle like these.

"I want to you see the kitchen," Tom said. "Fritz and Cornie and I stopped there about a week ago for syrup. But we swept through the state in less than a day, and that's too fast."

He remembered the house, although we came upon it from the

opposite direction; it was before we reached Pittsfield, the house on the right of the road and the barns on the left; a big house, turning brown-black from years without paint. The woman in blue gingham and darker blue apron opened the door.

"You were here before," she said to Tom.

"Yes. Can we buy some of that good maple sugar?"

"No objection."

She showed us what she had for sale. It was nothing in fancy packages or coy shapes such as roadside stands dote on. She offered pound blocks of maple sugar or plain boxes holding a pound of plain, oblong cakes. We each took a pound block, as suitable to our massive, masculine mood.

"Can I show my friend your kitchen?"

The woman looked us over. She was about sixty years old and had the loose-hanging arms and quick hands of a worker.

"If you like, why not?"

"I've been telling him it's the cleanest kitchen I ever saw in my life. It's a wonderful kitchen."

"I guess I like it clean." Her voice was pleased and proud. She led the way back through the house.

Her kitchen was large, perhaps twenty feet square. The massive, iron wood-range was polished black and its nickel-plated ornamentation shone. The linoleum floor gleamed spotless. There were white curtains on the windows through which sunlight flooded. The sink was clean and empty. A huge water barrel stood near the sink, and spring water flowed into it constantly from a lead pipe and out through an overflow pipe. The kitchen table was covered with red and white cloth. The shelves had clean china and glassware.

"Can we have a drink? I come from Brooklyn, and they don't have water like this."

She filled a dipper for Tom and then for me.

I told her I lived on a farm in Connecticut, and Tom explained we were writers and were out to see Vermont.

"Some folks travel," she said. "I never had need to go out of Vermont, except we went to Albany on our wedding trip, and I was down to Hartford once."

"It's certainly a wonderful kitchen, with that big stove; I'll bet it's warm in winter," I remarked.

"So long as the menfolks cut the wood, I'll keep them warm and fed."

At the front door she said she hoped we would come again.

"I'll never forget your kitchen," Tom said; and later, as we drove along, "She's a wonderful woman. That's the way to live."

Beyond the little village of Pittsfield we saw some men making a second cutting of hay in a flat shining meadow. It was such a sight of sunlit beauty that I neglected my watchfulness as driver, and nearly plunged us down a fifteen-foot terrace into the meadow. I yanked the car back onto the road just in time. That one scared Tom. I apologized.

"I don't think we would have been killed, but we sure would have been afoot."

"I'd have had us over sure, if I'd been driving. I wanted to grab something, but didn't know what to grab."

We turned back through the main range, climbing up through Brandon Gap on a dirt road, and stopped at Middlebury toward the end of day, found a place for the night, then, leaving the car, walked out to the campus of Middlebury College. We found some of the buildings open and went in to look around, reading notices on bulletin boards and confirming our opinion that colleges, in addition to the special spirit of each, have a college quality in common. Tom talked about the two colleges where he had been, and I talked about the two where I had been, and we agreed we liked the small ones best. The one where he had taught was something else.

"That was a factory," he said.

We saw one or two early students strolling in evening light on the campus, there about a week ahead of opening day. The evening was cool and cooling down more for one of those clear nights of early frost. As we stood on the bridge looking down at the dark swirl and plunge of thick waters over the dam and the fall that is practically under the main street, Tom decided he needed a warmer shirt.

"This one's used up, anyway. I ought to get me one like yours."

I was wearing a checked flannel shirt. He had on a white one, and he was right about its being used up. But when we looked around near the bridge and then toward the Green the clothing stores were closed.

When we got back to the hotel we could see some of the college buildings in black silhouette on their ridge, and a few separate trees still and dark, like pictured trees, against the far warmth of a late western sky.

The next morning we went to a dry-goods store. Nothing about it was new; it had served people for generations. It was long and narrow, with a high ceiling, goods laid on shelves that could be reached only by ladders. A dark-haired, black-eyed young girl, first startled at our tallness, tilted up a smiling face, ready to wait on us.

"My friend wants a shirt something like mine," I said.

She laid a pile of such shirts on the wooden counter, and we looked through them. I unpinned one and held it up to Tom's shoulders. We all three laughed.

"You'll have to do better than that," I told her.

"Gee, I don't know if I can. That's our biggest."

"Sure you can. Ethan Allen used to get his shirts here."

"Don't know him."

"A great big fellow. One of the Green Mountain Boys."

"Oh, you mean *him*. History. Wait a minute."

And she went to an office in the back of the store.

"I always have to go through something like this," Tom said, and was embarrassed at his size.

"They grow big ones in Vermont, too. You just wait."

The girl came forward with a grey-haired man who was at least five feet six inches tall. He looked up at us, and said to the girl, "Oh. I see what you mean."

First he looked at Tom, surveying his mass; then he stood there thinking for a moment. He looked toward several different sections of shelf space. Then he made a decision, came out from behind the counter, crossed the store toward the front, climbed a ladder, fetched a big box down from near the tin-covered ceiling, opened it on the counter, and revealed three red and black checked shirts. He unfolded one, shook it out, and reaching up held it to Tom's shoulders. The tails of that magnificent shirt swept down nearly to Tom's knees.

"Now you're talking," I said.

"Just what I want," Tom added.

"Made for you," the man agreed.

The dark-eyed girl watched us with delight.

We rushed back to our room with the shirt, in high spirits. Tom ripped off his used-up, whitish shirt, threw it in the wastebasket, and put on the warm, vast, and proper new shirt, of red and black checked flannel.

"They sure have fine people here in Vermont," he said.

A Picture of Thomas Wolfe

Neither he nor I knew how to improve the lower reaches of Vermont streams. They flowed in beds of naked, rounded rubble.

Work done by steam shovels and bulldozers to protect the roads had only made the stream beds look more naked.

"It would be useless to write our congressman," I said, "because we don't come from Vermont."

"And it's a Republican state," he added darkly.

But when we reached the edge of the mountains, where hoar-frost sparkled on fern and stone, and started up toward Ripton, Bread Loaf, and Middlebury Gap, the stream beside the road was beautiful. It turned and tumbled over brown and darker rock, it was crystalline and cold, dark hemlock boughs brushed above deep, ledge-confined pools, and moss and frosted flower waited on the brink for the touch of sunlight. We stopped one place to look longer, dabble our hands in a particular pool, and estimate the trout we would have caught had we brought rods, flies, and licenses. We got down on our hands and knees, then on our bellies for a drink; and Tom lingered a moment to have a good look at the reflection of his proud new shirt in quiet water. "That's a pretty good buy, for $2.78," he boasted.

"I've bought worse for more."

He didn't usually seem to like his clothes, but I think he liked that shirt.

We passed Bread Loaf, which now looked empty of conferring writers.

"I don't think anybody can teach anybody to write," Tom said.

"Read the magazines. Study the markets. Profit from rejections. Listen to editors. Maybe your paragraphs are too long. Maybe your story isn't slanted for the slicks!"

"I went through it in the playwriting course. Box office is God."

Both Tom and I lived to try to teach students to write. I know he lectured one summer at a writers' conference; I taught some courses at Columbia.

We must have done some doubling back, for we were climbing

the mountains again, from the west side, after noon, through Lincoln Gap. The crest of the Gap was sharp, and the dive of the road down toward Warren was steep. We soon ran into road gangs, building a new road up the steep eastern slope. There was grand activity in green shade and sunlight, with scrapers, bulldozers, dump trucks. Logs, stumps, and boulders were being shoved about, and the raw earth exposed. We inched along down narrow places or waited for some road machine to give us way. Some young men worked naked to the waist, but the older ones kept their shirts on. Wolfe tried to take it all in, the men, the machines, the views; I let a lot of it go, so as to keep the car on such road as there was. Thus we got down into Warren, where we looked for a place to eat. At the one house where there was a sign the lady told us we were too late for lunch; but she said if we would go up the road toward East Warren and turn right, there was a farm where they might feed us.

We decided to walk.

The stream that flows down off the East Warren flats into the Mad River at Warren, was just the kind of stream we both liked, and at one place, where it spread and tumbled down over a dark gleaming slant of ledge rock, we went out onto the rock between braidings of water, took off our shoes and socks, and washed our feet. Then we took snapshots of each other sitting there with water swirling around, and hemlocks in the background, and the dark rock of the mountains to sit upon.

Farther up the road we saw a man in a shed grooming a sorrel horse. Sunlight poured in upon them. It looked like a fine horse to us. Then we climbed the last steep stretch before the flat and, turning to look back, for the first time saw Lincoln Mountain in its full majesty. Precisely there, coming up out of the ravine, is the best spot I know for getting a sudden, impressive, and memorable sight of a Vermont mountain. I've been in Vermont every year now, one place and another, since 1930, and had many a sudden view, but none so astonishing as that. Tom stood there, legs apart, hands on his hips, face lifted, and looked his fill. We had Lincoln Mountain (4,013) devoured, all right; and such a good deed increased our appetite for lunch. We got up onto the flat, and strode along the open road, with a wide view of the Northfield mountains ahead, and Lincoln, Ellen, Stark, and Camel's Hump behind.

Presently there was a gay sound of trotting in the sunlight, and along came the man driving the sorrel horse hooked to a two-wheel trotting rig. We shouted, as the man went by, that it sure looked fast and he shouted back with considerable pleasure: "Is!"

I suppose he was getting his trotter ready for the races at the Rutland Fair.

We climbed a long hill and reached a farmhouse high in open fields, with big barns in front to shut off the winterblow from the north. The front face of the house was painted white, the east face red, and the back was not painted. We never saw the west face. A woman in a pink cotton dress came to the door.

"Well," she said, "my husband's working on the road over to Lincoln Gap. He took lunch along. I just got myself a bite a couple of hours ago. I don't know."

"We don't want much. Eggs, maybe."

"I've got eggs. Sit on the porch if you like. I'll call you."

"It's a grand view," Tom said.

"Yes. Off up in the mowing to the right there, you'll find a pile of rocks. If you go up there, you can see Mount Mansfield." She looked north, a long way. "It's clear. You'll see that far today."

We sat on the porch with plenty to fill our roving eyes until she called us in for our snack. She charged us fifty cents each, and provided ham and eggs, boiled potatoes, coffee, bread, butter, milk, jam, and pie. She felt the price might seem high, but hoped the size of the portions made up for it.

"I got to thinking at the stove, you two are pretty big men. So I made the extra eggs and got out the pie."

We went up into the mowing to the pile of rocks to smoke and look. I suppose, in a straight line of vision it was forty miles to Mt. Mansfield. We saw that, all right, and saw Madonna Peak and Morse Mountain five or ten miles farther on. The mountains stretched too far away to show up in a snapshot, and for that reason we took pictures of each other on the pile of rocks.

Because all the snapshots from that trip are now lost, I had better describe Tom as he looked to me there and then. He stood upon a conical pile of rounded stones which had been ploughed out of the earth and were weather-washed. He wore brown trousers and his great torso was swathed in that splendid new red and black shirt. The breeze toyed with his dark hair, for he wore no hat. There was a ruddy flush on his face. His brows were relaxed. His eyes, full of a thousand gorgeous playings of light from the valley and the ranges, were steady, steadfast, and luminous. He was not smiling; neither was he looking truculent or tormented. His mouth was at rest; he was breathing slowly, deeply, awake and poised and beholding a vast spread of earth with majestic calm joy. His hands were great hands, idle at his sides in comfort.

All the nearby grass was gilded by the sun. The near mowing shone green; the near mountains rose dark, massive, and firm; sun was upon distant houses in the width and tumult of the valley; the far mountains sparkled blue; the gentle, radiant clouds drifted through the spaces of sky. His whole heroic figure had glowing outlines of sunlight. And all the mountain fragrant air was filled with the great music of the wild and living earth. There he stood, man of mountains, man of earth, man of sunlit sky, upright Man himself, in splendor, alive with amazing intelligence, gazing about the world in radiant poise of quiet joy.

A *Little Woman*

We walked gossiping along three or four miles of dusty road. Tom thought he ought to get himself a small place in these parts, where he could settle down quietly to finish his book.

"And I need a nice little wife, too."

"Now you don't want too much land," I warned him. "It comes in big pieces, and when you see it spread out in evening sunlight, it's hard to resist. But if you get more than one acre, you'll have problems. Fences, brush, and the horrid temptation to do 'just a little farming.' You'll never finish the book. And the woman better not be too small. I warn you, Tom, a little wife takes a lot of looking after. The little ones leap and dart and are born just to wind big men around their pinkies."

"Well, she's going to be a good cook, and she's going to raise vegetables and chickens and hams and bacons . . ."

"And little Wolfes."

"Ha!" He leapt in the road for joy.

Toward sunset, driving north, as we neared a bridge we saw a "For Sale" sign nailed on a tree in front of a little house.

"Do you want that one?" I asked, slowing down.

He looked it over from the road. The maples were big above it; it had a couple of small red barns; sunlight glowed on a hillock of sere grass behind the barns. The windows of the house looked cool and dark and quiet.

"Yes. I'll take it."

"Once you've got the house, you'll have no trouble at all finding the little woman. But ask her if she can typewrite."

I stopped the car, then backed it, then turned into the farmyard. We knocked at the front door and presently heard a man's voice calling from around the house by the kitchen door.

A neat, slight man, about sixty years old, or sixty-five, was at the back. His overalls were clean and neat; his blue shirt was clean and neat. His face was clean, and his fringe of grey hair was combed smooth. He had a small, trim, grey mustache and clear blue eyes. There was a quiet sadness in his face.

I explained that we had seen his sign and that my friend wanted to get some idea of how much a place like this would cost. I said he was a writer, who lived in Brooklyn, and wondered if he could afford a place in the country.

"I came from Staten Island myself, fourteen years ago," the owner told us. "Me and the Missus. This is just about the right size for one man. Twelve acres. Your own cow and chickens wouldn't take too much time, and you'd have the rest of the day for writing. I'll show you the barns first."

In the first small barn he showed us a little Jersey cow. He patted the cow's flank and spoke to her in friendly tones, and she turned her mild face to contemplate him. She had neat horns.

"I've milked her tonight and had my supper before you came in. The evenings are long now for me. My married son wants me to come back to Staten Island. We had this place, she and I, fourteen years together."

The other little barn held hay, and there was a chicken house with Rhode Island Reds bunching up for the night.

He took us back to the house and into the kitchen. Tom had made many friendly and pleased comments on what he had seen, especially the late sunlight on the hill of sere grass behind the barn; and he and the sweet-tempered man exchanged lore of Brooklyn, Staten Island, and the great harbor of the great city. Our host by now had estimated that we were visitors rather than purchasers, and we paused every few steps, and in each room, to hold a little conversation.

The kitchen was clean, but very still. "She always kept things clean," he said. "I keep it that way now."

He showed us the dining room and the living room. There was a front porch shutting off some of the outdoor light, so that the living room was dim. A small rocking chair, with a curved wooden seat and flowers painted on the arms, stood near the fireplace.

"That's her chair," the man told us gently. "The last months I would carry her from her bed and set her in the chair, and there she would pass the day. She never complained." He looked up at us. Tom, especially, nearly touched the ceiling with his head.

"She was a little thing," the old man said, "but she was a great one to suffer." The three of us exchanged the quick, deep, and solacing glance of brotherhood.

Driving on toward Montpelier we talked of him all the way, saying to each other as well as we could that our lives had been enriched; both Tom and I knew that the man out of his open heart had given us a great gift.

The lights were on in Montpelier. We passed a number of houses with tourist signs and finally stopped at a big brick building on a busy street, where we got a room with a bath. It was not a hotel, and yet it was not a private home. About twenty people had rooms there, a few for the night, but most of them steadily. There was something approaching Y.M.C.A. atmosphere about the place. There were typewritten rules for guests posted in the bathroom and in the hall.

Later in the evening Tom said he wanted to write a letter to his mother (I think his mother amazed him). There was a room on the first floor for general use, and he sat at a varnished, yellowish table there, and wrote a letter to his mother. He spread his arms wide on the table as he wrote, and he did not dash the letter off, but rather wrote it calmly and slowly.

When I read this letter, ten years later and five years after his death (on pages 263–264 of the published volume of letters to his mother), I thought it was one of the most nearly happy letters he wrote to her; and reading it, I remembered many pleasant, companionable things about him.

The Ultimate Reduction of Vermont

Although we had taken the capital city of the state on September 13, at nightfall, we did not rest on our laurels, but the next day carried town after town and mountain after mountain, reaching St. Albans at nightfall, replete. From that position we felt we had cut off the northeast corner of the state, and left it for subsequent warriors to mop up.

We stayed in the Tavern in St. Albans, did some rechecking on our road maps to tick off cities, towns, villages, and mountains we had devoured, and schemed our return in such wise as to reduce other salients. We would bypass Calvin Coolidge's Plymouth, in order to make a frontal assault on the sector around White River Junction, for from those parts came Maxwell E. Perkins, and Wolfe had a personal interest in capturing the Perkins country by eye storm.

We retired to a big room to study our guidebooks, but, as usual, talked instead, largely of boyhood. I cannot say that Wolfe lay on his right side like a lion, like Buddha, in that composed posture of great and ready strength; but rather he lay on his back, his head propped on pillows, his hands clasped behind his head, and a toe sticking through a sock, in that open-eyed posture of one who is dreaming worlds.

We went out for breakfast to a narrow restaurant across the street from the park; we sat at a table against a dark bluish-green wall; and I remember that place with sadness because I happened to go in there alone for breakfast one morning some years later, and when I sat alone at the table against the dark bluish-green wall and opened the newspaper I had brought over from the Tavern, I read the tragic news that Thomas Wolfe had died.

We had reduced Mt. Mansfield from the south, from the east, from the west, and now we took it from the north. I stopped the car at the crest of Smuggler's Notch. Tom opened the map.

"We've sure ravaged the state of Vermont of its Piddling Hills, Tom. But there's Jay Peak and Ascutney Mountain left. Shall we let them keep those?"

"Not both, Bob. What do they need with two mountains? We'll lap up Ascutney, and leave them Jay."

While we were sweeping up the Perkins country, down around White River Junction, Tom noticed that more farmhouses than usual were built of brick. These houses looked compact, impregnable, and secure on the ground.

"I might have known Max came from a section like this," he said. "If Vermont is solid, this is the most solid part of it, and he is the most solid Vermonter ever born. Why, it took Coolidge a whole word to say 'yes' or to say 'no', but Max can do either without a sound. Just look at that brick house, Bob, under those big maples; a hurricane couldn't make it tremble. That's Max."

We stopped at a place for cider and got some that was hard, which was our only strong drink on the trip.

Our last night in Vermont was spent in Wallingford, in a room remarkable for its beds; this was a "mansion," where a widow now took overnight guests. There were glass-fronted cases of Victorian books in the wide hall, a walnut stairway with a curved bannister, and in the room we had, two double beds built of walnut. The smaller of these two beds was larger than the average double bed, and the larger one was the only bed I have ever seen built for a man the size of Thomas Wolfe. One was on one side of the room, and one on the other, with plenty of space between their foot-boards. We lay propped on pillows, looking across the room at

each other, and exchanged choice bits of information and guid-
ance, he out of the Shakespeare book, I out of the Montaigne. We
didn't make much use of Aeschylus on that journey.

Then he laid aside the book and said to me a poem of his own,
somewhat like this:

"This is a wonderful country, Bob. I would lie in some narrow
room in England or France or Germany, with the odor of ancient
darkness on the walls, and remember the fresh air and light of
America, perhaps those iron railings along a board walk by the
sea, which no other country has the same, or our great trains
aburst with fat produce, stroking across the massive breast of our
land, or our place names chorded with the music of all races of
man; and then I would come home to America again, to the violent
streets, and shake with pain, desire, frustration; and then would
come the vision and break of light; out of the secret, inward darkness, from under the welter and web of greed, lust, power, evil,
violence, would flow up and radiate that true light from the soul
of America, more generous, free, healthy, humane, and healing
than the light any former nation has cast upon the world."

We had our breakfast next morning at The True Temper Inn,
our last breakfast together in Vermont, a hearty, friendly breakfast
in a good name-place.

On October 9, Wolfe wrote me a letter from his new address,
5 Montague Terrace, Brooklyn, beginning:

Thanks very much for the pictures and for the drawing [a water-color
sketch I had made from memory and sent to him] of my favorite house
—at least, that's what I took it to be. Since it came on my birthday, I
thank you again for remembering me.

I have thought of our trip a hundred times and like it better every
time I think of it—[11]

It is almost incredible that I should have insulted him, to the
point of rage, before snow fell.

[11] Unpublished letter, October 9, 1933.

8. THE CRISIS

Thirty years have passed since I precipitated the crisis in our friendship, and I still remember the sombre pain and spiritual toil of that night as one of the depths of my life, made all the harder because of the cold and grimy place where it began, along about midnight. It was on a Thursday in the last week in October.

After our good trip to Vermont, which had surely deepened our affection for one another, I had resumed work on my third novel, *Fortune*. But Wolfe had several weeks of nonproductive distress. A sufficient cause for his not writing was the fact that he moved from his place on Brooklyn Heights to a new place nearby at 5 Montague Terrace. The new room, he said, was bigger than the old, and cheaper, too. He wrote me his telephone number, which was unlisted, asked me to phone him if I came to town, but not to give the number out to anybody—"unless it's an heiress." Then I got another letter from him: he had begun writing again, at top speed, and felt better for it; he was worried about his sister in Washington, who was ill; and he was trying to arrange a meeting between me and his friend and editor, Maxwell Perkins.

I had wanted to meet Perkins, and Tom wanted me to meet him; we had talked about it while driving through the Perkins country in Vermont. But it turned out that it could not be arranged during that October.

However, on the last Thursday in the month I went in to New York. I met Tom out on the sidewalk in front of Scribner's, we had dinner together and went to a theatre. I do not remember the play, but we had seats far up in the balcony, and neither of us was comfortable, for there was not room for our legs, and our knees were jammed against the sharp tops of the seats in front of us, and we both knew the above-average height of our heads bothered the people behind us. It was a relief to get out and swing along in the October night toward the Lexington Avenue subway.

After we crossed Fifth Avenue, which has an air of wide and leisurely quiet late at night, we decided to have some coffee and went down a flight of steps into one of those underground cafeterias that are joined to the vast buried warrens of the subways. Neither daylight nor fresh air ever reaches them. I have never been in one that was really clean. The most you can hope for in the way of cleanliness is that someone tired and soiled, slapping a soiled wet rag, may wipe your tabletop of the dribblings of a former occupant and that perhaps a weary little man with a mop or a broom may be cleaning the floor in streaks and patches. Such places seem never to close, never to be full, and never to be empty; the coffee boiler is always steaming, the same food is always lying in warm masses on the counter, and the grease-coated exhaust fan is always drawing out grimy air above the short-order grill and the hot plates.

The one we entered was small. The floor was paved with something hard, grey, and cold; the walls were tiled in white with gritty dust on them and the ceiling, in the yellow light, which yet glared on the tiles, was a sickly green. The tables had hard white

vitreous tops, like the hard whiteness of a bathtub. We got ourselves each a cup of coffee and some doughnuts and sat at a table
to eat and talk. I used some paper napkins to clean off some
crumbs and coffee splotches left by an earlier visitor. Tom lit a
cigaret and looked around. I filled and lit my pipe. We both kept
on our hats. Sitting in the small chair at the little white table he
looked out of place, and so, perhaps, did I. The room was too
little, the ceiling too low, the table and chairs too small. The half-
dozen other people in there were the little underground people of
New York, tired, small, brooding and exasperated people, with the
dogged courage of primordial man to hang onto life and live it
out. It was always easy for me to understand Tom's sympathy for
Gulliver among the Lilliputians.

Tom was talking about the sorry schism between himself and
what might be called the Lilliputian literati. His face was warm
and troubled. I knew the sort of people he meant. They congre-
gate in New York; they write reviews; they work on magazines, in
literary agencies, or for publishers; or in some way set themselves
up in the arts. Fundamentally they are not creative, neither creative in business (like a fine editor or fine agent) nor creative in
the arts (like a fine critic or a good writer); but they make and
hold their reputations by surmounting the reputations of others.
They so conceive their own superiority that they can tell you the
flaw in any good thing, from a clear cry of the heart to a masterpiece, or from a child to God. This year they tear down the idols
they set up last year.

"I know what you mean, Tom, though I scarcely suffer from it
myself. When my first novel was published, it was damned by a
few of these notables, and not even considered by the rest, so that
I have never been set up in their Pantheon. So far as their wits are
concerned, I do not exist to be toyed with and torn. But you are a
thorn and a challenge to their uncreative rapacity."

"They talk. They write their niggardly hints. 'What's happened to Wolfe?' 'Wolfe burned out in one book.' You meet them at a party, and one of them says, 'Oh, yes. So-and-so was telling me about you the other day—' What? Good God, what? You close yourself in your room in Brooklyn and squeeze the blood out of your guts and soul for all the terror and truth that's in you, and these jackals whine and whisper behind your back and wait to paw over your entrails. What are they saying? Good God, what are they saying now?"

This was the point for me to find and say a healing and creative word. Tom was troubled and hurt, but he was not angry; the thing at the moment was not biting deep with the horror he sometimes felt. I should perhaps have suggested one of Dante's rings of Hell for the backbiters, or at least I should have pointed out the sound poetic splendor of some of the pieces of Tom's writing that were appearing in *Scribner's Magazine,* fragments more full of life than many another man's whole novel. But instead I consorted with the jackals myself. With the naïveté of a child I took his question— "Good God, what are they saying?"—as a plain enquiry rather than as a rhetorical outcry. I answered it.

"I'll tell you the kind of things they're saying, Tom. Before I ever met you, one of them was talking to me about you." I told him about the little man in the literary agency. "He said you sure liked your liquor. That's the measly kind of thing they say."

When I was a boy in New Mexico I would often stand on a cliff in the mountains and push a big stone over the edge. After the instant when the stone toppled off the brink, there would be a prolonged moment of tense and expectant silence; then the stone would thud onto a ledge below, dislodge other stones, and start a rumbling of rock down a rock-cluttered slope, and an odor of sparks and sulphur would come up, mingled with an odor of pine forest. Finally a grown man told me this was a damn fool thing to do—did I want to start a landslide?

By a spiritual analogy it was just such a thing that I had now done to my friend. I had pushed a dark, heavy, and ugly stone over the brink of one of the cliffs of his soul. There was a prolonged and dreadful moment of expectant silence during which the troubled warmth of his face hardened into a hot, sick, and staring anger. Slowly his full underlip began to push out beyond his upper lip and his marvelous deep and dark eyes stared at me with crescent loathing from under the shadowy brim of his well-tugged brown hat. He said nothing. The anger and loathing in his expression broke up into a horror of demoralized and painful sickness, and he could no longer bear to look at me. He silently drained his cup of coffee, set it down, slowly crushed out the fire and by a kind of slow horrible pressure burst the paper of his cigaret in the saucer. In the dead silence between us there was a Miltonic awe and majesty, as of a soul toppling from some brink of heaven, "With hideous ruin and combustion down / To bottomless perdition." Such great motions of the poets describe true happenings in the soul, and out of the knowing of Milton or Homer a man better understands himself and his friend.

I was not God and Tom was not Satan, and one man should not do this to another. But the grandeur of his vulnerability was part of the greatness of his creative soul. Wolfe was a man of myriad-webbed earth, nurtured on the great thoughts of man's uncounted generations of spiritual aspiration, and the happenings in his soul had the splendor and tragedy of ultimates. For he, too, was a poet.

He said, in a voice of brooding and nauseous misery: "A man thinks he has a friend he can trust—and then that friend talks behind his back."

He stared down at his broken cigaret, which was turning wet

with coffee in the saucer. I smoked my pipe and watched him, ashamed of what I had done, and took the pipe from my mouth, sick of its taste and beginning to feel oppressed by the disgusting odors of stale food and bad air. But I was still naive. I thought he meant he had been betrayed by the little man who had gossiped about him long ago to me and behind his back, and not by me who repeated the words to his face. Then in a resurgence of anger his lower lip swelled out again, he lifted his head, and he looked directly into my eyes for one instant of hot fury and loathing. To me this was a blow of great violence, far more powerful and shocking than the most bitter words, for words, after all, are symbols and substitutes for spiritual communication, and no word of love or hate has the overwhelming power of a direct glance out of the soul. Once in my youth, when I worked at a coal mine, a powerful man stood in a tremor of hatred before me and spoke a few bitter words meant to rot my soul, and while he spoke there burned in his eyes the hot and furious desire to murder me. If he had not spoken he might well have killed me. Tom's look was devoid of murder, but its unspoken sickness and loathing said with all the might of his pain and rage that I was the friend he had thought he could trust, but who had betrayed him.

I was frightened. I felt a chill of loss and disaster. I had not talked about him behind his back, but I had committed the great folly of repeating a scandal about him to his face. In the common way of things, when you say a man likes his liquor you indicate a shallowness, a loss of center, and a certain quality of irresponsible despair in that man's life that simply were not true of Wolfe. He was not shallow, he labored prodigiously to find and hold and create from center, and he fought despair to the last ditch of agony and had the recreating power of hope until the day of his death. If now and then he indulged in the anodyne of drink, it was certainly not a giving up of life implied in the phrase "he likes his liquor." Tom had enormous knowledge of common meanings, and it may have seemed to him that I was telling him to his face that he was giving up life.

He gave his hat a tug and said with a miserable finality, "I'm going home."

At the same time he rose to his towering height. Before he could turn his back on me and stride away, I too stood up and said,

"O.K. Let's go."

I could see a quick shock of fright in his face before he turned his massive back on me. It was as if he had cried out, "Good God! Have not my words and my sickness, horror, and loathing put an end to this monstrous betrayal!"

Quite clear in my mind about what I was going to do but unaware of how hard it was going to be to do it, I followed him with my own unspoken words, "I know you and I love you. I will not let you do this to yourself or to me. Our friendship shall not be broken here and now."

I think if I had spoken these words aloud he might well have turned on me with a cry of rage. At the moment I was so profoundly to him an enemy—The Enemy—that any further word acknowledging, explaining, or hoping to mitigate the crisis would have been the death of our friendship.

He was too proud to run from my loathly presence, but he had a giant stride as he fled out of that miserable cafeteria and down along the dim and sterile corridors toward the subway. My stride was equal to his, and I kept beside him through the dead corridors, out under the great arched ceiling of Grand Central, across the vast floor, and on down into the subway. Neither of us said a word. I let him go first through the turnstile and followed him on down more stairs to the subway platform. We stood there in the dark draft of night waiting for a train. He turned his back on me. I was clearly conscious that this was a most painful thing that I was doing, but it had to be done. The train came, we got in, and I sat beside him.

I generally look at and see a number of different people when I ride the subway. There in the tunnelled noise and yellow light of a hurtling train I have received uncounted revelations of dim and profound meanings of life in the flow of its eternal moments through the bodies and faces and beings of strangers. But all I remember of that haunting, long, and painful ride to Brooklyn is that the car was but pleasantly filled and warmed by people, with several seat spaces empty and a few people standing out of preference; that, and Thomas Wolfe seated on my left, on the left-hand bench. He would not look at me. He would not speak to me. I could hear his breathing, sharp and snorty. I could see the side of his face and one eye, his fine clear nose and truculently stuck-out lower lip. His cheek was flushed and looked hot.

At moments I felt I was doing a servile crawl and self-abasement to appease a childish and unreasonable fury in my friend. I do not like anger between people, and I was not above being a servile coward to stop it. I knew also, however, that I was capable of a cold pride that would let a man go on his own terms if he so desired. This present emotion was different. It was neither crawly cowardice nor cold pride. This was a plain and silent assertion of affection. This was a downright silent insistence upon justice in love between friends. I had committed a folly and Tom had mistrusted my love, and it would not have been just for either of us to destroy our friendship because of that. I did not know what else to do but stick it out, hoping the silent affirmation of my continued presence would restore his confidence that I was in truth his friend. It seemed to me that I heard a million thuds of the wheels on the rails and that every breath he snorted out told me I was an abomination at this side. I stuck it out.

We came up out of those desolate tunnels of night onto the

night streets of Brooklyn, strode wordless side by side, saw the night towers of Manhattan, dark and aspiring against the sky, but winking with lights, and came to the door of the narrow housefront among housefronts where he lived.

At last he turned his face to give me a look which said "Goodbye," but without sound.

"I want to come up and see the new place you live in," I said.

He went in the door and started climbing stairs in a poorly lit, narrow, and dingy hallway. I followed a step behind him. Not I, but hospitality, got hold of him on the way up the stairs to his private door. He opened the door and let me in. The room was dark. There was only a dim light from outdoors coming in through the front windows. He turned on a light, looked at me with sullen acquiescence, and threw his hat across the room. It would have been wrong to expect him to endure any more. Neither could I do any more.

"It's late, Tom. I have to be getting back. But I did want to see the place where you live now."

He paced back and forth. Now and then he smashed his big right fist into the big palm of his left hand, but rather sorrowfully than violently.

This new room, like the one where I had visited him before, was also, in a way, heartbreaking. It was larger than the other and with a high ceiling. In spite of the clutter of packing cases full of manuscript, shabby and broken furniture, heaped and shelved books, a writing table and some unwashed coffee cups and saucers, it was a bare room, a homeless room, a lonely, shut-off cave of compulsive, solitary, and prodigious labor. For whatever reasons of all his life, Tom had never developed any aesthetic sense or power by which to use materials and objects to create a sheltering and spiritual beauty in the place where he lived. His life was naked there.

"You are a good man, Tom. I must go now."

He stopped pacing and looked at me from the back end of the room, tall, massive, in dim light near the rear wall.

"Good night, Bob."

I opened the door and started out. Then he strode toward the door, grasped the inner knob in his left hand, and reached out his right hand for me to shake, gradually closing the door between us as he did so, for I already stood in the hall. His face in the closing aperture of the door was in dim light, but there was light enough for me to see his expression, and it made his face beautiful. It was an expression of very quiet remembrance and very sweet peace. It was as young and as beautiful an expression as I ever saw on his face. The grip of our hands together was firm and strong as we shook them several times up and down.

"We had a good time in Vermont together, Bob. I'll never forget our good trip to Vermont together."

"We did. And I'll see you again."

We made a last squeeze and shake of hands and let go. He finished closing the door, slowly and softly, and I went down the stairs.

To hear each other's voice, to see one another's face—we cannot be men without that. I had not quit, nor let him quit, short of being a man. Before we parted, we saw, we spoke.

I could not bear the subway yet. I walked across Brooklyn Bridge. Out on the bridge, up in the clear sweep of October night, between island and island of the water-wound City, I shivered; and it was not outward cold so much as inward tremor and aftershock, the shock of a catastrophe barely avoided.

There on the arch of the Bridge (a flash of memory made the old Bridge a symbolic bridge between Tom's life and mine; I saw it first as a thin spright child in Santa Fe, pictured on a postcard that my father and oldest brother, good, courageous Jim, who at the age of twelve, when Father died, became with straight cour-

age the man of our family, brought back from a trip to New York—
they had walked on it!—and I had lived to walk across it many
times, as Tom in his days and nights had also done)—on the noble
old Bridge arched over the dark river in the midnight wind of
October, between the wharfs and vast agglomerate of Brooklyn
and the slums and towers of Manhattan, it occurred to me what
was the profound difference between my friend and me. I was
frail-born, not expected by doctor or parents to live out that day,
and lay often in a coma, blue and still, for many months; and Tom
was born, like the infant Hercules, for labors vast and huge. To
me it was a miracle of God to live at all, to him a tragedy of man
not to conquer life. "Tom feels he is large enough to conquer life,
and I feel that life is large enough to let me in. That makes it
easier for me than it will ever be for him to know that we are less
than God."

For how can there be any love between friends or love between
two persons unless one of them, or both, knows that we are less
than God?

9. THE MOTTLED SKY

On a night when the sky was mottled, Wolfe, a dark tall giant in a long dark coat, made tracks in fields of snow out around our house, and by means of what might be called symbolic reverberations he summed up the troubles of mistrust there had been between us.

I do not know German, but Tom knew it well, and sometimes quoted Goethe's lyric of yearning for the warm south:

"Kennst du das Land wo die Zitronen blühn . . . ?" But he also knew that haunting line from Villon,

"Mais où sont les nieges d'antan?"

There can be no doubt that on the night of December 31 of that year and on into the early hours of the New Year there was a mottled sky over this part of earth, with a moon shining through and snow covering all the fields around our house. Where are the snows of yesteryear?—and where are the tracks he made that night in the soft clean snow of the old year? After an outburst of his petulance frightened Marguerite into the house, I was the only one who saw him. I saw his tracks in the snow leading up to where he stood alone on a mound of white—tall, dark, and gesticulating in the shadowy moonlight.

I had invited him to spend Christmas with us, and he had written he would like to come, especially because it had been years since he had celebrated Christmas in a home where there were children. (Now, all these years later, there are grandchildren here, too; and two of my grandchildren have already this morning come into my study and been amused to watch me writing this; I told them what I was writing, so that my friend Tom might be honored in my house unto the third generation, and so that my grandchildren should know what concerned the heart of their grandfather that day; they watched me solemnly while I wrote about a hundred words, then ran off to other glee.) It was touch and go whether he could come out for New Year's Eve. I understood by now that Thomas Wolfe always had an advance engagement with the present, when and whatever that present might become. Usually it became solitude and work, for work in solitude was the dominant engagement of his life. However, toward evening of December 31 he telephoned from New Canaan, where he had been spending the day with the Perkins family, to ask if he could come on up. He said he could catch a bus to Danbury, if I would meet him there.

The children were in bed, and I left Marguerite reading in the living room when I drove over to Danbury to meet him. The night was mild and moonlit, with a soft blowing of clouds, and the cleared highway was quite black among fields of snow and snowy woods. Tom had been sitting near the middle of the bus; he greeted me through the window and then followed other passengers out. They got out easily, but he had to maneuver his hugeness out of the narrow door. He carried his forever bulging and battered brown briefcase. He wore a long dark coat and his old brown hat. He had on a sort of moss-grey suit, which Marguerite still remembers as being very handsome—she remembers his suits were of good material and good tailoring.

There was a kind of shrewd and expectant chortling in the way he greeted me. He and Perkins and I had recently had our first dinner together, in clear and friendly candor, and I was surprised now by the glint of cunning in his mood.

I knew almost at once as I started driving home with him that I had a problem of petulance to handle. Though he did not say a word about it, I felt certain that my damned quotation of gossip still irked him, and something truculent and saucy in his manner seemed to say, "I'll show Bob whether I like my liquor or not!" He was not drunk—I never saw him what I would call drunk— but he was high. He had been drinking at the Perkins' house, and he was in a mood of satirical irritation with women. Wives in particular, but all women.

We left the black highway for the snow-packed dirt road and came to our house. Marguerite opened the door and greeted us. Tom dumped his briefcase, coat, and hat on a chair in the hall, and we all sat down in the living room. Tom sat on the green couch, near the end table with a lamp on it. He looked tired and mussed. Youth had, I think, come near its end in him; there were moments when some light of remembrance or a new instant of perception lit up his face as with a flash of youthful vigor; but on the whole he was utterly weary, passing out of a youth of prodigious strain and poetic production into a maturity haunted by death.

It was nearing midnight, and I wanted very much for Marguerite and Tom and me to welcome the New Year with a drink together. Since our marriage we had had two bottles of strong liquor in the house. The first was a bottle of applejack, given to us when we signed the deed to our house in Newtown by the Polish farmer from whom we bought it. He had made the applejack himself, and he and I each had a stiff drink of it to close the deal. That bottle had been finished during the past year. But one of Marguerite's brothers had given her a pint of fine Scotch whiskey for Christmas. Marguerite and I had each had a drink from it, and I had had another. Our drinks had been small, and the pint bottle was nearly full. I brought out this bottle, with glasses, ice, and water, and poured three drinks. Marguerite fundamentally dislikes the taste of liquor and was slow with her drink, but Tom gulped down his first, and my second accompanied his third. I could see that Marguerite was distressed at this male swallowing-up of her Christmas gift, which she had expected would last a long time. (Nowadays we are accustomed to serving liquor in our house and to receiving it when we go out; but then this was new to us.) When the clock struck midnight we drank health and Happy New Year to one another; then Tom, pouring whiskey on ice, without water, finished the bottle.

I had not had time or means to let Marguerite know that Tom was on the warpath, but she realized he was being defiant, for he dwelt in his moods and made no effort to conceal them, and his mood of irritated cunning was as plain that night as, at other times, had been his moods of joy and candor.

She suggested that we get the sleds and go coasting on the slope behind the grey barn. She and the children had been coasting out there that afternoon. She said it would be lovely now in the moonlight. We had several ordinary sleds and one quite large one on the porch.

We put on our warm coats and hats and gloves. Marguerite and I put on galoshes. Unfortunately I had no overshoes large enough for Tom to wear; but he said he didn't mind going in his shoes.

It really was lovely under the cloud drift in the moonlight, and for about half an hour we talked and laughed and shouted, coasting down the hill, pulling up our sleds and coasting down again, pausing to look at the night, at the barn roof and pine trees against the sky, at the snowy slopes of the field with brush or a rock sticking above the snow here and there, glancing at the silent bare trees down in the swamp and at the woodland-blackened ridge off to the west, then coasting again. Then, by a mischance in slamming my sled at the top of the slope, I jolted my sacroiliac and went back to the house intending to lie on the floor and get it back into place again by a method the doctor had taught me. I said it would be too uncomfortable for me to coast any more, and I would wait in the house for Tom and Marguerite.

As I started pulling my sled away, I heard Marguerite challenge Tom, "I'll bet I can slide farther than you!" I went on toward the lights of the house, and they started down the hill.

Then presently I heard Tom's voice, loud, sharp and accusing, followed by silence. I stood, waiting for another sound, and Marguerite came up alone from behind the barn, through the stone fence, wearing a red scarf and a black fur hat, pulling her sled with a hand in a red mitten. She had on her short black fur coat. When she reached me her almost always rosy face was very white. At that moment we heard Tom yell at the sky down in the field.

"What's the matter?"

"He accused me of planning the whole thing. He said I only challenged him because it was my coasting hill and I knew how to beat him. Then he cursed me."

"He's having revenge tonight. I'll go see what I can do."

"Your back?"

"I can manage."

Marguerite went on into the house. I left my sled near the lighted window and returned to the coasting hill. I saw Tom's big sled in the snow at the foot of the hill but I did not see him. Then I heard him yell at the night, and saw him on the mounded edge

of our little sand pit, down near the schoolhouse where I wrote my
novels. His back was to me. He was tossing his arms and yelping
with loud animal vigor. He was like a dark giant at primitive rejoicing in the fields of snow.

I had nearly reached him before he turned and saw me. He
leered at me and yelled again. Then he said, "Come on, Bob. Yell.
Are you afraid to yell?"

He made loud shouts, explosive and reverberant. In boyhood
I had learned two kinds of howling. One, supposed to be an
Indian shout, both to carry and to echo, with a slow beginning and
a deep, sharp ending, I had learned on a camping trip in a canyon
among the cliff dwellings (where scientists at Los Alamos now
prepare worse noises); the other was a coyote wail I had learned
on the prairies of Nebraska and Wyoming. Tom's yell I took to be
native to some wild humor of his Smoky Mountains.

I let out a couple of howls, and we howled in disharmonic union.
Then Tom looked at me and looked at the sky over our head, and
he challenged me,

"All right, Bob. What epithet would you choose to describe that
sky up there tonight?"

I put my hands on my hips and looked up at the sky. There was
a web and flowing of soft grey clouds, the undersides almost black
in splotches, the edges moonlit, and all moving from southwest to
northeast in a mild wind. Occasionally the moon shone through,
and through any break stars could be seen. I was about to choose
an epithet, when the word "epithet" itself gave me warning. I suddenly realized that I had insulted him with that very word "epithet" in the review I had written of his first novel, before I had ever
met him. He was summing up accounts tonight, and remembering
that four-year-old insult. For in the review of his book, although
I had written things that rejoiced him and had compared him as a
writer with Whitman and Melville, I had gone on to say, with

Lilliput conceit, that in Wolfe's work we did not find the perfection of epithet that we found in *Moby Dick*. Ah, the silliness of reviewers and the vanity of authors! A reviewer must cringe and die unless he assert his superiority by finding some flaw in whatever masterpiece; and an author must cringe and die at anything less than unadulterated adulation.

"Gee, Tom," I said, "I wouldn't know what to call that sky."

"What epithet would Browning use?"

I shook my head. "Browning would be stumped."

"What epithet would Keats use?"

"Keats would go home and think about it."

"What about Melville, ha? How about him?"

"Poor old Melville would be at a loss."

He swept a great arm across the flow of heaven with its clouds and moon and stars.

"I'll tell you something, Bob. Wolfe calls that a mottled sky. Old Tom Wolfe knows his epithets."

"He certainly does. It certainly is a mottled sky."

Then he began to shout and whoop, and I joined in with a coyote's howl.

When we finished and took breath, there came across the silence from a quarter of a mile away a woman's shout from an upstairs window,

"Shut up! Go to bed!"

The night was still, and her voice was clear. Tom answered it with another yell. Again she cried out,

"Go to bed! Let people sleep!"

"I know a good place for yelling, up on the hill, Tom. Let's go."

"What's the matter?" he leered at me. "Are you afraid of your neighbors?" And he yelled again.

"She gets up at dawn to milk her cows," I said. "Let's let her sleep."

We heard her final cry of "Shut up!" and heard her bang her window shut.

Tom muttered and chortled at my pusillanimous fear of neighbors, but he went along with me. We trampled and shouted our way up through several soft and snowy fields, until we stood on a high, clear place in the third field beyond and above our house, and yelled out first my lungs and then his. In lulls between howls we looked round about over the valley below us, down at our house, down at the distant neighbor's house and at the rim of all the hills under the flowing clouds and light of the mottled sky. I had not had so long and good a yell-out in years.

When we came home to bed, Marguerite was already asleep, and in the morning Tom apologized to her for his rudeness, and we had a jolly breakfast with all the children.

In the afternoon we went over to visit Martin Lewis in his studio, and especially for Tom's interest Martin showed us a number of his watercolors, lithographs, and etchings. The work of Martin Lewis is a new creation in the great tradition of Goya and Rembrandt, and he in his pictures, like Wolfe in his pages, reveals rich and sombre wonders of human life in the great city. They understood each other well, and all the better because Martin's seasoned and compassionate maturity was able to comprehend the strenuous overstrain of Tom's youth. I was glad they liked each other, for I liked them both.

A while later, from Brooklyn, Tom wrote, saying:

Ever since I came back from New Year's at your place I've wanted to write you and Marguerite and tell you how good it was to be with you New Year's and how it set me up. I am sorry that you have seen me so often just after I've been through the sausage mill. I suppose one should want to see the people he likes best when he is sitting astride of his own world, but instinct in me seems to turn me toward the Raynolds family for succor every time I begin to wander around in the valley of despair. I won't do it again, or not very often, and before I go away I swear I will reveal to you all the noble Jekyllesque side of my nature.[12]

I don't know where he thought he was going, for I believe he stayed in Brooklyn for months, bound to labor on his ceaseless book.

[12] *Letters of Thomas Wolfe*, pp. 404–405.

10. REPEATED PLEASURE

Repeated pleasure is at the heart of friendship.

I think men make friendships in a venturesome spirit of creating something new; but a friendship once firmly founded is prolonged and endures on a basis of repetition; order, meaning, and value are elements in this repetition, and if the order is liberal, the meaning hopeful, and the value good, the desire for repetition endures. Tom and I no longer expected much that was new in our relationship, but we were confident of mutual affection, confirmation, and hope in repeated communion. Each of us had the same old thing to give again, a large simplicity of understanding; there had not been and there was not going to be any spiritual stealing, the one from the other. This was a good friendship to have achieved in an age of anxiety, mistrust, and spiritual thieving. Each time we met I felt a larger, warmer, and freer sense of being, which was his continual gift to me; and I believe that each time we met I somehow gave him renewed confidence in his worth and in his work. And there was a deep thing we recognized and honored in one another, which was that each of us was spiritually committed to a high and ultimate seriousness in our work. This was a religious commitment, at the heart of poetry.

The repetitions of the pleasure and richness of friendship are, however, better for a limited than for a fulsome telling. For that reason, and before I write of my meetings with Max Perkins and Wolfe together, I wish to summarize several years in our friendship by recounting three of the vivid memories I have of seeing Tom very much alive, one in Newtown, one in Scribner's office in New York, and one when I lay in a hospital bed.

Gettysbury and Fountain's Abbey

He was in the last year of the most stupendous labor of his life. For years now he had referred to "the manuscript" or "the book" as one refers to the central engagement of one's life. By one count this was the fifth year of his long toil on *Of Time and the River,* though I believe he sometimes counted it seven years and very often counted it forever. He was so thoroughly engaged—brains, bowels, and soul—in the living and creation of the book that the labor was not only finishing the book but was also concluding his youth and threatening his life. I believe the same thing happened to Melville when he wrote *Moby Dick,* and perhaps to Tolstoy when he wrote *War and Peace.* Tom had accepted the total challenge to find and express what he was: he would write it down though it killed him; and he would never be the same again.

I got a letter from him, written on July 8, 1934, in which he announced:

It seems unbelievable, but Perkins and I finished getting the manuscript ready for the printer last night. There are still three full scenes to be written, and parts of a few other scenes to be completed, but he wants to start getting the stuff to the printer at once. As for myself, I am fighting against an overwhelming reluctance to let it go. There are so many things I want to go back over and fill in and revise, and all my beautiful notes I long to chink in somehow, and he is doing his best to restrain me in these designs.[13]

Having seen them together now several times, I could easily imagine the adamantine quietness with which Perkins would say, "No more, Tom. The time has come."

Martin Lewis had an analogy for it. I was in Martin's studio one afternoon watching him pull a trial proof of an etching. He saw a place where he thought he had overworked the plate and said with the humor of grim knowledge, "It takes two men to produce a work of art, one to paint it and the other to hit him over the head just before he spoils it."

Meantime I was writing the last pages of my novel *Fortune*. I had sent Tom a copy of what I intended as a dedication page, and he thanked me for wanting to dedicate the novel to him.

All at once I was through writing the book, and Marguerite and I went for a Sunday morning walk in a glen where hemlocks grow. It was a lovely morning among the great trees, with ledges of rock at our right and a stream down below on our left.

"This smells like the forests in Germany," Marguerite said. "I wish you could have a trip to Europe."

"Let's go."

It took us ten days to arrange for a good friend to stay with the children and get our passage and passports; Tom came down to the ship to see us off. During a week in Germany, where I smelled the heather and the forest, we saw Hitler fifteen feet away, got spiritually sick of "Heil Hitler!" and were glad to go to England for a month.

Tom had directed us to one of our loveliest pleasures in England. He had come to Newtown for several days with us before we sailed. He and I took some good long walks round the countryside,

---

[13] *Letters of Thomas Wolfe*, pp. 416–417.

in the fullness of summer, with the great good black dog Storm bounding and loping beside us, behind us, before us. Once when we came back, hot and cheerful, Tom lay at full length on the green sofa, and I sat talking with him; a five-year-old daughter came into the room, walked over to Tom, looked at him in grave silence for a moment, then said,

"You smell."

This was the last trial-by-insult ever to take place between Tom and my family. He turned his large head, gave the child a startled glance, and she stepped back a pace.

"We all smell," I said to the little girl. "You'd better go find the other children, because Uncle Tom and I are busy talking."

She gave Tom a steady look, one of certainty in her impression, her dilated nostrils verifying her sense of smell, then turned and wandered out of the room in her own depth of silent thought.

Tom's nostrils dilated, too, and there was a look of distress on his face. His shirt was sweaty from our walk, and he hunched a big damp shoulder over against his nose to sniff at it.

"Let me tell you, Tom, about the first time I learned that I could smell. It was a shock, and a healthy enlightenment. It was back about 1921. I was working at a coal mine out in Colorado. Part of my job was to give out orders for blasting powder to the miners. They would come out of the pit in their stinking clothes after a heavy day of sweaty labor, and my fine young Princetonian nostrils were offended at their stench as they stood before me while I filled out their powder slips. Well, then, it happened that a few months later I transferred from the mine office to a labor job on the tipple, where in heat and dust and noise and oily grime I handled heavy mine cars all day long, until my work clothes were saturated with weeks of sweat; then one day, at the end of work, walking toward the wash-house, in a pocket of still air, I caught a whiff of myself. 'My God,' I thought, 'I stink, too!' The shock did more than two years at Princeton to make me feel a part of humanity, and I've felt more deeply human ever since."

Tom smiled at me, then he sighed.

"I forget everything. I know nothing, except the book, for months at a time. But the end is in sight. Galleys will start coming in this week. We hope for publication in November. I've turned down some good offers for parts of it for magazines, because I feel I owe it to Perkins not to take any cream off of publication of the book itself."

That evening, sometimes lying on the couch with a great arm crooked under the back of his dark head, and sometimes rising to stride in our living room (which, fortunately for me too, because I often pace as I think, is more than thirty feet long) he told Marguerite and me about a recent trip he had made into Pennsylvania. Partly because I had lived in Easton, where my mother still lived, and had finished college at Lafayette, he had stopped for a while there to get a feel and taste of the town which had been home to a friend. (I am sorry that it was not until after his death that I visited Asheville, where he had grown up.) He talked about the wild and wooded country where he had been visiting as a guest at a home for defective children. Seeing these children had shocked his heart. But Pennsylvania is a good long word referring to large reaches of earth and referring to regions where he had also searched for his father (even as among the marbles of Vermont), and presently, with a joyous glow on his face, he was talking about the farm lands out towards Gettysburg, the fat farms, the fat orchards, the fat-to-bursting barns, and the wholesome and huge-eating farmer folk he had met out there. It was one of those radiant moments when Wolfe, the talker, happy in his listeners, poured forth the good speech of direct and joyous experience. It was not touched by the darkness and anguish of spiritual toil that often moved his writing into tragic depths. Both Marguerite and

I could rejoice with him, for we, too, had visited the broad and fat farmlands of Pennsylvania.

Then we got to talking about our suddenly planned trip to Europe and our decision to spend the major part of our time in England, because Marguerite wanted to show me, even more than the forests of Germany, the brown grandeurs of Dartmoor, and we both wanted to see English cathedrals. Tom then began to tell us of things he had seen and places he had enjoyed in England. The two above all that he said we must not miss were Hogarth's painting of the heads of his servants, and Fountains Abbey.

Quite possibly Tom's gift of an expectant pleasure in visiting Fountains Abbey was one of the thrusts that urged me into five years of writing plays. He described the ruins and the park with such pleasure and vividness that we made our plans to include the north of England. So it happened that we got as far as Durham, where the Depression was harsh, the mines mostly closed, and the people on dole. Added to my own experience of a coal mine was this stark view of a mining community, dominated by a great cathedral, and suffering human disaster, so that I wrote a sort of ballad, which I called "The Song of the Ugly Runts," and which, when I sent a copy (I can't remember why) to J. B. Priestley, he called a "grim set of verses." Then, soon, I read in the papers about a group of miners in Hungary who shut themselves in their mine and threatened mass suicide, unless their conditions were bettered. Out of these three things, my own experience of a coal mine, the Depression in Durham, and the tragic story from Hungary, I wrote my first poetic drama, *The Ugly Runts,* and went on for five years writing plays. But it was certainly thanks to Tom that we stopped off in Lincoln, where I had the good fortune one afternoon to be in the cathedral while the organist played Bach's B Minor Prelude and Fugue; and thanks to Tom we spent a full day and went back for part of another day at Fountains Abbey. There is a warm loveliness in those clean old stones and a great peace in the park and woods, the memory of which I still cherish as one of Tom's good gifts to me. And the strong Hogarth painting in London I remember still.

And I had need of comfort stored in the spirit, for when we reached home I was met with the minor bad news that Harper had rejected *Fortune*, and with the shock of news that my mother was dying.

I had received at least one long letter from Tom while I was in Europe. He spoke of his longing, as he had when he talked with us, to go to Europe again, and especially to revisit Germany. But there could be no far travel for him until the book was done. He wrote that he had already been given more than a hundred galleys of proof. Publication of *Of Time and the River* was at last in sight. He expressed his mood in a sentence:

"It reads wonderfully well; they all seem to believe in it."

At Scribner's

Wolfe asked me to come see him in the editorial office at Scribner's on Fifth Avenue. I was more nearly at the end of my emotional tether than I knew, and so, I believe, was he.

In the four and a half months since returning from Europe I had achieved a positive work of considerable force, in the writing of my first play, *The Ugly Runts*. (Having seen it produced, with Tom Powers, Jessie Royce Landis, Estelle Winwood, and Paul McGrath in leading roles, I know, not alone from my response, but from that of audiences and critics, that on the stage it is a poetic drama of considerable power, and I have often regretted that Tom never saw it, for I believe he would have been deeply moved by that piece of work. It is slanted toward God, not toward the political left, and never reached Broadway.) I had, however, to my own shame, been at work on a despoiling revision of *Fortune*, in response to editorial suggestions, so that that novel as finally published—and dedicated to Thomas Wolfe—was a mutilation of a better work I had done. I was sick of what I was doing to *Fortune,* knowing at bottom that the guilt for debasing the work was my own. Finally, during those months I had been often at my mother's bedside in Easton, until her death in January from the destroying action of a series of strokes.

Meanwhile Tom had at last finished "the book," and was preparing to sail for Europe in advance of its publication. How dreadfully he had bruised and wounded his tremendous life on the anvil of his passionate labor may be judged from a letter he wrote me a few weeks later from Europe, in which he said:

> . . . was in Paris for a little more than two weeks after landing—a very bad two weeks, for I couldn't eat or sleep and there are three days which are almost a total blank—i.e. I have no ordered memory of them and for me that is almost the most horrible form of experience . . .[14]

I met him there in Scribner's office. At that time you came out of the elevator into a fairly large inside room (called the library, I believe) which had some chairs, a big bare table or two, and a number of bookcases, some of them forming alcoves. Private offices with windows on Fifth Avenue were partitioned off in the front of the building, and I think there were others to the rear. But Tom was in this central room when I got out of the elevator. He came forward to shake my hand. Perhaps it was the poor light that caused it, but his face seemed softened and discolored with exhaustion. But he was excited and his eyes were lit up with a kind of glee, the glee a boy has when he takes you by the hand and says, "Now let me show you something wonderful!" Tom, indeed, took me by the hand, led me to a big table, and asked me to sit down. He stood beside me.

[14] Unpublished letter, March 29, 1935.

"Bob," he said, "you sit there. I have a surprise for you. You just wait a minute, I have a surprise for you."

As he said this he was taking a pen from his pocket. Then he went off behind my back where there was a wall of bookshelves and another table. I was not supposed to look, but I could hear him stirring behind me there. Then he came back, and I stood up to face him. He held something in a hand behind him.

"Bob, I'm proud to give you this," he said, and bringing his hand from behind his back he made me a gift of a brand new solid and heavy book. It had a paper jacket of various greens in wave-like design, and white lettering. His thumb held the front cover open, and taking the book I read what he had written in ink that was still wet, filling the whole blank page opposite the front cover:

> For my friend
> Bob Raynolds
> with the earnest hope
> that this book will
> do nothing to diminish
> a faith, a friendship
> and a belief
> that have meant more to me
> than I can here put
> down— Tom Wolfe
> Feb 13, 1935

The bold lettering on the front of the green jacket read:

of

time

and

the river

THOMAS WOLFE

AUTHOR OF LOOK HOMEWARD, ANGEL

I shook his hand and smiled and grinned and thanked him, and he shook my hand and grinned and smiled. We looked into each other's eyes and forgave one another for not being able to say what we knew; and more deeply said it by our silent trust.

But even as I stood there clasping his hand, our eyes in communion, I both wept and rejoiced within, "My friend has broken his life to make this book. It would have killed a lesser man. No lesser man would have dared or could have done it."

His youth was dead. Thomas Wolfe was never a young man again.

Hospital and Ship's Sailing

On the morning of the day he sailed for Europe, Tom came to see me in the Lenox Hill Hospital. Mrs. Jelliffe came with him, and they brought me a large bunch of gladioli of that soft coral or sandy vermillion flush that I have loved since childhood as one of the warm colors in old Navajo blankets and sandstone cliffs and, sometimes, in hollyhocks against an adobe wall. Mrs. Jelliffe was breathless and rejoicing in a kind of impatience, for, through some error, they had first tried to find me by going into the clinic building on Seventy-seventh Street. They had been told I was not in the Hospital. Finally someone advised them to go around to the Seventy-sixth Street entrance and try the private wards. And so, with rushing and dashing—and she was a tall woman, as strongly bred of the Southern mountains as Tom, and capable of rushing and dashing with him—they found me. She enjoyed it all more than he did, for he was appalled at seeing me in a hospital bed and wearing a plaster cast from my waist and down one leg nearly to the knee. My little buxom Irish nurse added to his discomfort by repeating a joke she and I had evoked about the situation, "We're going to keep Mr. Raynolds in that thing until he gets mouldy."

Mrs. Jelliffe, who was the widow of a doctor, realized that the cast was so much apparatus and that the patient was in no particular need of sympathy; and I tried to explain to Tom that the "operation" was not really an operation; the doctor had done some pulling, hauling, and readjusting of my legs and back and then had slapped and wound this cast about me to hold my sacroiliac bones immobilized until they got properly firmed in place. But Tom still didn't like that cast.

On the table beside the bed were the three books I was reading: Aeschylus, Milton, and Wolfe. The Wolfe was the heaviest. I reached for it and opened it and showed Tom how I could rest its weight on the upper edge of the cast and so read it in comfort.

"Look, Tom. I'm one of your first readers. I'm liking what I read, and thanks to this plaster cast I'm going to lie here reading your book without straining my wrists."

"He's right, Tom. You know your books weigh a ton at the end of an hour's reading," Mrs. Jelliffe told him.

Well, he couldn't stay long. He was sailing in a few hours now. But he did want to see me, and he thought he should have come before. I was sorry I could not go down to the ship to see him off, but Marguerite planned to be there and wish him bon voyage for both of us.

"Have a good trip, Tom. You've more than earned it. And don't you worry about your book. I've been reading it here in the company of Aeschylus and Milton, and in their company it doesn't let me down, which believe me is a mighty good book. Perkins is going to send you some good cables when it comes out."

He stood tall and grave beside my bed, looking down at me with a quiet warmth of friendship, asked me to write him, and hoped I would be up on my feet soon.

Each of us knew how profoundly tired the other was, and each of us was comforted by the friendship between us. I was pleased that he had come to see me, and I saw him go with, as it were, a warm shadow of my affection following him. When Marguerite

came that evening she said, "Tom looked splendid, waving from
the ship."

I read the Aeschylus, the Milton, and the Wolfe there in the hospital; and each of the three speaks affirmative knowing of the
tragic grandeur of man. I wrote him a sonnet on his book.

> Not Prometheus had so proud a tongue,
> Nor felt from vulture's beak more bitter woe;
> Apollo never was so mad, so young
> Nor made of mortal more immortal throe;
> Foam-wreathed Poseidon swayed a calmer sea,
> And patient Ceres gleaned more gentle earth,
> Venus wove less strenuous mystery,
> And Bacchus' ruddy grapes spilled easier mirth;
> For these were gods of ancient sunny hills,
> And he is poet forged by wilderness;
> Their forms and smiles replied to fated ills,
> His joy is torn from dark, flame-fissured stress:
>   Heaven again, new trust of God, is won like this,
>   When mortal ranges hell, still seeking bliss.

But Thomas Wolfe was never to be young again. He prowled the
streets of Paris in despair, despite my sonnet and Max's cabled
praise; he could not sleep, felt overwhelmed with shame, went to
hear the celebration of Mass a dozen times in Sacre Coeur. So he
went to England (whence he wrote me of that black horror of lost
memory of days in Paris) and to Denmark and to Germany. And
that summer, with his book done and his youth dead, he saw in
Germany horrors of political and social insanity destroying the
decencies of human life.

In the several years left of his life I never again saw a splendid
look of radiant youth light up his face. I shall tell, as well as I can,
what I did see. But first I want to tell what I know about Wolfe
and Perkins as I saw them together.

11. THOMAS WOLFE AND MAXWELL PERKINS— MEN OF HIGH ORDER

The most obvious thing about Maxwell Perkins was the high quality of his character. Perkins and Wolfe were quite wonderful together, for Wolfe, too, was a human being of a very high order. In almost every way that could be apprehended by the senses— their size, their coloring, their manner of speech, the felt quality of their presence—the contrast between them was dramatic. Wolfe was an unusually tall and massive man, while Perkins was slender and of no more than medium height; Wolfe was fundamentally brunette and Perkins blond; you saw the fleshy contours of Wolfe's face and the bony structure of Perkins' face; Wolfe was loquacious and eloquent, Perkins succinct and penetrating. Wolfe would say, "Max is laconic," and Perkins would say, "That's one of Tom's dithyrambs." They watched each other with surprise and affection. The warm, luminous brown eyes of Thomas Wolfe and the "sea-pale," illumined blue eyes of Maxwell Perkins watched each other with a very deep affection.

I experienced a lifting up of my spirit each time I met with them. To be in the presence of persons of a very high order does lift up my spirit.

Sometimes during the last year of their work on Tom's book I would meet them about six-thirty P.M. up on the fifth floor of the Scribner's building, in Perkins' office. The first time I did this I thought they were ready to go out and that I was late, for when I arrived Perkins was wearing his hat. I soon learned that he liked to wear his hat in the office. He would sit in his chair at his desk, tip the chair back toward the wall, and look up at you from under the brim of his hat. I would call his place there a plain, rather bare, and modest office, with good clear light coming through the window. It was large enough for one quiet man to do his work; it became full when two were in it. When I entered and found both Perkins and Wolfe there, it was then too crowded for work.

For some months it was Tom's custom to go to Perkins' office at four-thirty, when the editorial routine of the day was finished, and work there with Perkins for two hours. At other times, by night, they would meet either at Perkins' New York house or at Tom's room in Brooklyn, and Tom sometimes took his manuscript-fattened briefcase out to Perkins' place in Connecticut. I came upon them several times in the office just as they were folding up work for the evening and saw such things as galleys, scissors, and paste being put away, saw piles of typescript and some of those bound ledger books in which Tom wrote so much. I cannot say that I ever watched them at their work, in the sense of seeing them actually cut, revise, select. And yet in the sense that counted most I did watch them at their work, for the physically invisible process of creative work going on between two men may be spiritually apprehended by one who knows and watches them together. Men of the high human order of Wolfe and Perkins do not cease the quiet inner labors of creation when they fold up a few papers for the night. The work still goes on in every glance between them.

If it was winter, Perkins would turn out the light and we would find the library and other offices dark and empty while we rang and waited for the elevator. The air of having been deserted for the night gives offices a quality by which you feel they are not of basic human importance. They are tools, of secondary usage and compulsion in our lives. When you see an office deserted at night you somehow know that the human beings were glad to abandon it. Most of them only came there and worked there through the day for the sake of other things in other places.

On the street people often glanced a second time at the three of us walking together, with the top of Perkins' hat reaching about to my eye-level but only to the lower line of Tom's jaw. Perkins made us appear more strikingly tall than when it was just Tom and I walking together. Out among street noises and without a clear and direct view of the speaker's face, Perkins often missed what Tom and I were saying, and our walks on the street were in the nature of getting quickly somewhere to a quiet table where we could sit down and talk together. But while walking I noticed that Perkins as well as Wolfe was a great gatherer of information about the flow of life around him. If I saw something remarkable, such as a stenographer going home late with a copy of *An American Tragedy* hugged under her arm, or a plume of steam catching the last glow of sunlight above a tall building—yes, Perkins had seen it too, and so had Tom, and each of them had known how to understand it within the texture of a rich associative fund of knowledge about human life in the city. The fact that I, too, was quick and various at seeing was one of the things that brought me within the field of their communion; but when the three of us were together it was always true that the profound intimacy, the deepest communion, the primary friendship was between Perkins and Wolfe. Through some inborn generosity they never made me feel excluded but rather made me feel welcome as a fresh and agreeable fact in their mutual world.

I recognized that both Perkins and Wolfe had a clearer sense of commitment to this present world than I. As one who often feels like eternity's alien in any present, I admired them for their direct and capable participation in the stress of the contemporary scene. They were definitely recognizable as effective modern men. I do not believe that either of them thought of me as an effective modern man. In the eternal wonder of living at all, I could not forget the eternal tragedy of being a man. They felt the difference and allowed for it, as if perhaps my devotion to other rhythms of time had human value, too. I shall try to make understandable, near the end of this work, the source and nature of this profound difference as between Wolfe and myself.

Sometimes the three of us had dinner together. I remember one summer evening when we went into the basement of an apartment house over on the East River, and from there out onto a barge tied up against the river wall and fitted out as a restaurant. It was a fine bright evening with a fresh breeze after a hot day. The tables were set under an awning, which made the outer air seem the more bright. We heard shouts and splashing, and looked over the rail, where we saw half a dozen lithe, sun-browned boys swimming in the dark and glistening upstream flood of the tide. We had some drinks, then ate and talked for two hours. From time to time the conversation would come back to "Tom's book." That was the central subject on their minds long after the day's overt work on it was done. To write down the vast total of recollected life was on Tom's mind, and to help Tom shape a book from that huge and still growing agglomerate was on Perkins' mind. Each understood and respected the purpose of the other; each held to his own purpose, and within six or eight months of that evening there were to be both a large and rich published book and a still growing, written-down record of recollected life. Writing it down, forever repeated, forever endless, forever new, was Wolfe's function; and getting Wolfe to shape a book in the midst of the torrent was Perkins' function; and both of them did their work.

On a number of occasions when I was in the city, perhaps for a dinner with Marguerite's family, I would meet them for cocktails in a small cocktail lounge on a sidestreet near Scribner's office. I remember that at that place we were served little grilled sausages on toothpicks, and I always gobbled half a dozen of them with my several drinks. Wolfe and Perkins would rise to greet me when I came in, I would join them at a small table, and we would talk there and sip our drinks with our heads close together. On one of those occasions there was a question going between them about the effort being made by some persons to persuade Wolfe to join the Communist Party, or at least to become a fellow traveller.

"Tom," Max teased, "is not the one who should be the radical. He's never really been exploited. All through school and college he had money from home. I'm the one who worked my way as a wage slave all along the line."

Tom gave his friend a brooding look, but his smile was close under it.

"Neither of you," I suggested, "is sick enough of life, or so frightened of it, as to become a Communist. Your religion is open at the end, and all your saints are outside any exclusive church."

I remember them seated there, in the rather dim light affected by such places, each of them on the verge of a smile, regarding one another with a quiet and deep affection.

I have survived both men for some years now, and I have often meditated with warmth and with affection upon my memories of them.

I believe Maxwell Perkins was aware of and held in reverence some radiant center in the manifestations of life, and that he was always watching for the direct ray from center. He was an illuminated man. He was a man of deep-founded balance of intelligence and integrity. He was a quiet, patient, unselfish and fearless worker who restored and increased the grace of human life. Perkins was a personal man; he spoke right to you and listened with fully receptive intelligence for all the truth in you. He was a man from whom I always received the gifts of courtesy, clear and direct attention, and an unconcealed expression of his own thought about and response to the vitality of what might be under consideration at the moment. In the presence of Perkins I felt, and still remember, the experience of meeting a man of very high personal order.

I have heard much quibble and gabble about whether or not Wolfe could ever have written a book at all without Perkins to help him. Such quibble and gabble, coming like poison into Wolfe's oversensitive ears, was part of the cause of an outward hiatus in their friendship. It has also been used to bolster up the new, corruptive fashion of editorial revision of any book that comes to hand. I wish I could throw some new light on this situation in justice to the memory of those two men. I am going to try to do it.

Wolfe, in his little book *The Story of a Novel,* has fully attested to the large fact of their years of working together which resulted in the publication of his novel *Of Time and the River.* I believe the ultimate literary fact about Thomas Wolfe is that he had a mighty creative power and used it with courage and faithfulness to produce a large body of poetic work. I believe that the ultimate human fact about Maxwell Perkins during those five years of labor is that he worked with a man, Thomas Wolfe, rather than that he worked on a book. Wolfe was a master of poetic creation, and Perkins was a master in human love. Perkins helped the wild heart of Wolfe, pouring out its torrential response to life, to hold steady through the years of exhausting and titanic labor. I can believe that without the steady love and watchful, wise illumination of his friend Perkins that Wolfe might have killed himself by these labors (as, in fact, even with Perkins on guard, the work did hasten his death); I can also believe that without Perkins' help, Wolfe would still have confessed his tremendous heart until he died, whether it ever got printed in books or not.

The deepest fact is not literary at all. It is the ultimate human fact that the two men loved each other, and that love enlarged, ennobled, and made more fruitful each of their lives. Perkins was a just man, rapidly; Wolfe was a just man, more slowly. And although there came later what appeared to be a tragic break in their friendship, this break was not ultimate. It was Perkins above all others whom Wolfe wanted with him when he was dying; and it was Perkins who came to Wolfe's deathbed. I know that Wolfe loved Perkins as long as he lived; and I know that Perkins grieved at the death of Wolfe, whom he loved.

12. A GOOD MAN: END AND ETERNAL

Last Times in Brooklyn

For a moment, while reading his story, I had the feeling that my friend was eternal. We had often talked about William Blake's poetry, and Tom had more than once picked up a volume and, with his liking for concrete evidence of what he was discussing, had read aloud to me that strange and magic creation of Blake: "The Tiger." Each time he read this poem to me aloud, his voice deepened with the wonder of a man who is offering his own heart in words; and I felt that he knew the poem about the tiger was also an everlasting portrait of Thomas Wolfe. It was Marguerite who had first put Blake's poetry in my hands, soon after we were married, and when the children were very small she encouraged them to memorize some of those magic songs, so that they came to have for me a rich complex of personal association with my wife, my children, and with my friend Tom. And "The Tiger," especially, was Tom. It was for these persons, really, that I wrote a lyric of few lines celebrating Blake's power to fill a stillness around each

word with music. I sent Tom a copy, because he admired this
power of pure lyric word in Blake, in Keats—so opposite to the
passionate flood of his own music. That may have been one of the
reasons why he asked me to read the story he had written. In the
years that I knew him it was rare that he asked anyone, except of
course his editor or agent, to read anything he had freshly written.
I am sure the story I speak of will be remembered by many, and
by these comments on Blake I am only trying to make more specific and full the deep wonder I felt as I read the story; for while
I read it Blake's immortal tiger, made into the mortal man who
wrote the story, was prowling back and forth in the cage of his
Brooklyn room.

Here, then, is William Blake's prophetic portrait of Thomas
Wolfe:

> Tiger! Tiger! burning bright
> In the forests of the night,
> What immortal hand or eye
> Could frame thy fearful symmetry?

For Thomas Wolfe knew Blake's Tiger was also wild incalcu-
lable man, was also himself, and was the Negro he was writing
about in the story he handed me to read, which he called "Child
By Tiger." I sat on an open packing case, nearly full of his ledgers
and manuscripts, with these manuscripts for my cushion and the
edge of the box pressing against the undersides of my legs, and
read the story while he prowled the room. He wanted to know if I
thought it was good. I think he also wanted to defy those shallow
carpers who went about saying, "Wolfe? What formless verbosity!
The man couldn't write a story that is a story."

What I felt as I read "Child By Tiger" (later it was published
in the *Saturday Evening Post* in substantially the same text as I
read that night in a slanting light from under a green shade)—
what I felt was that my friend was eternal, that the creative eternal

which framed the awful symmetry of the tiger and of man suffused Thomas Wolfe's mortal heart and great and human frame
of being.

What I said when I looked up from the end of the story and saw
him prowling there with a cigaret afire in his lips was much more
simple.

"Tom, it's a good story. It's a wonderful piece of writing, with
dramatic and tragic form."

He stood a moment with his hands on his hips looking down at
me, then raised his big right hand to take his cigaret from his
lips.

"I can write a story," he said.

He smiled, but his smile was tired. His eyes were tired. There
was something heavier and laxer in the splendid symmetry of his
huge human figure. The light in the room was not strong, but even
so I could see a tiredness, a heaviness, and an unhealthy color in
the contours of his face. My friend was mortal. Thomas Wolfe, so
powerfully suffused in his time and in his being with eternal creative power, would never be young again and was going to die.

And there was a new weight of deathly shock bearing him down
since his trip to Europe in that spring and summer of 1935. He
discussed it with me and with Marguerite one of the last times
I saw him in Brooklyn, and the only time Marguerite saw him
there.

We drove in from Connecticut and over to Brooklyn at evening
especially to see him. The three of us had dinner together in a
nearby restaurant, then came back to his room for coffee and conversation. Tom smoked cigarets; I smoked my pipe; Marguerite
never smokes. In all of our tripartite conversations I was listener
and occasional commentator, for both Tom and Marguerite far
exceeded me in the spontaneous and outspoken talent of poetic
conversation. Each of them had a wonderful memoried store of

people seen living, and talked vividly about actual persons in the stir and crisis of life.

A good portion of the talk that night related to the tragedies and horrors burgeoning in Germany. Tom had been for weeks in Berlin, and only the year before Marguerite and I had visited for a week in a small German town near Hamburg. Tom may have seen Hitler himself in Berlin; Marguerite and I had seen him on the street in Hamburg.

Marguerite described, and I confirmed, the incident of how we happened to be standing on one of Hamburg's main streets when a thin line of storm troopers stretched along the curbing at each side of the street and then several automobiles came by, with Hitler standing up bareheaded in one of them, not a big man, with that shock of black hair.

"The surprising thing," Marguerite said, "was to see that his eyes were blue. I had always thought of them as being dark."

The surprising thing, I thought and said, was how that night, while we were having dinner with a group of people in a fashionable restaurant, everyone there fell silent, stopped eating, stopped drinking their wine—our own champagne went flat—to listen to Hitler speaking over the radio. Marguerite told stories of individual persons and how they behaved in the town we had visited; and I recalled being on a street in Hanover long after dark and watching a group of children come in from the country, so late, carrying shovels like guns and marching in order like soldiers.

Tom had a thing to tell us, of the steady and shocking apprehension he had had in Berlin of Germany ruined, of man corrupted, of the beast emerging first in politics and then rotting the whole social fabric. This was the new weight of deathly shock that bore on him the rest of his life. Much of what he told us he wrote out and published in a magazine article, and more or less the same telling was published again after his death in his final novel. When he wrote it he told me he was going to publish it, that he had to publish it, although he believed it would ruin his reputation in Germany and keep him from returning to that country, which he loved. The publication of the article temporarily increased his reputation among left-wing intellectuals in America; but (after his death) when the Hitler-Stalin pact was signed, these same left-wing intellectuals rediscerned him as a mongrel and debased enemy. And he certainly made it clear in his final novel that he abhorred communism as well as fascism.

For, I believe, the deathly shock Thomas Wolfe received that summer in Germany, directly seeing, tasting, touching, smelling the corrupt wickedness that flows from man's deification of himself, was the shock of perceiving that man cannot be the autarch of his destiny. He tasted that summer in Germany the dead-sea fruit of the absence of God; he took it to his bowels and knew it was poison. He perceived the ruinous lie at the heart of that ancient word-symbol of human wilfulness, "aut caesar aut nullus"; for in Germany, where it was a statement of the freedom of the human will to create its own destiny, he saw the concrete evidence that man deified and nihilism are inseparable; and the symbol was written, in the history of our time, in the ruin of men. Having believed Neitzsche's dictum that "God is dead," the Germans had deified themselves and gone mad.

It is my belief that during the rest of his life, and at least partly because of this shock of spiritual recognition, Wolfe tried less to capture the meaning of life in the burning Absence at the core of memory, and tried more to find that meaning in a sought-for apprehension of the Presence of God.

When I say that I believe Thomas Wolfe had now consciously become a religious poet in search of God, it is a hard saying and it is a passionate saying. I do not mean it in the orthodox sense of harking back to the medieval fold of Christian faith, or in the forlorn sense of shopping about among world religions for a comfortable God. I mean it in the hard and passionate primordial sense of the human soul face to face with the huge and horrifying darkness of non-being, the original and final sense in which there can be no spiritual sanity for a man and there can be no meaning in human life without a felt experience of the presence of God. For a modern there is no greater challenge and no more strenuous trial in the solitudes of the soul. As a modern man, Wolfe, like most of the rest of us in the Western world of today, was highly educated as a mechanic and enormously undereducated as a religious man. Science, technology, blueprints, constitutions, plans, organizations, percentages, statistics, polls—and God misconceived as an infantile or primitive illusion. For three and a half centuries we have been learning method without meaning and technique without spirit and wilfulness without God. Wolfe, in Germany, saw full fruit of this learning, saw the disintegration of the human soul sickening modern man. Knowing now the insanity of Absence, he sought on for the sanity of Presence. I do not know of a harder, or of a more passionate, or of a more needful thing than this for a poet to do, that he shall try to help us find our living God again. Nothing less than this will save our lives.

In outward ways it showed in his deeper loneliness. He had found his youth closed out forever; he was no longer in thrall to romanticism, the illusion that man is the creator of himself and his world and the conqueror of life; he was humble; he was the creature, trying to fulfill a good human life, not the creator creating it; he was, in his own words, which he used for the title of a noble essay, God's Lonely Man. More and more the fellowship of his final lonely years was with the great tragic and religious spirits who have spoken out of the sort of knowledge of human life that St. Paul had when he wrote to the Romans: "For tribulation worketh patience; and patience experience; and experience hope." This hope is quite different from youth's wild hope of gathering outward prizes from the world. This is the deeply founded inward hope of wisdom and compassion, which is illuminated by a sense of God. The Old Testament, the great Greek dramatists, the New Testament, the Shakespeare of the tragedies (particularly of *King Lear*—"Tom's a-cold . . ."), Dostoevski: these were the spiritual companions of his final years.

On one of the last times he visited us in Newtown he got to talking about *The Brothers Karamazov*; he thought it the greatest novel he knew; he wanted us to hear the end. I brought him Marguerite's copy from the bookcase, and he read to us the final chapter, particularly for the sake of Alyosha's talk to the boys at Ilusha's funeral.

For, having seen the wickedness of spiritual arrogance at work in massive historical actuality of fear, suspicion, hatred, and cruelty— and we who survived him by a few years saw it grow monstrously worse—now he knew the full importance of Christ's teaching of love, even as simplified for a specific moment in Alyosha's talk to the boys at Ilusha's funeral.

On the flyleaf of *From Death to Morning*, one of the last of his books that he gave me, he wrote in part to thank me for having dedicated to him my by-then published novel *Fortune*; but he wrote in a way that set a higher value on love itself than on any imperfect act expressing love.

Dear Bob—the greatest honor you ever did me was to be my friend—the next greatest was to dedicate to me a book in which you had put some of the beauty, passion and aspiration of your experience— All I can here do or say is to tell you I am proud and happy to owe you this great debt—and to hope that here—in this short book—and in my later ones—you may find increasing justification for your faith, your friendship, and belief— Tom

The Last Time I Saw Thomas Wolfe

In 1936 Wolfe left Brooklyn and came to live in Manhattan. He took an apartment on First Avenue in the Fifties, a block or two from where Marguerite and I had lived one winter, and both of us talked to him about how wonderful it was to be near the river there, where you could see the gorgeousness of garbage scows being tugged in sunlight or could go down at night to talk with harbor-men who had tied up their craft for an hour at the quay. It was the first time he had had a place in a building with an elevator, and he jested about such plush living—not even bedbugs or cockroaches!

I met him there several times, and once saw the basis for one of the odd legends about him. He was so big, some people said, that he wrote on top of the icebox. In that apartment there was a kitchenette with a small refrigerator. The top of it was at elbow height for Tom. I came in toward evening. He had a typist at work at the table in his living room, and he himself was writing with pencil on yellow sheets on top of that dwarf refrigerator. He just wanted to finish a sheet or two of the day's work before the typist left; and with the direct sanity of a good workman he was using the best available space as a standing desk for his work.

But of these various times before the last time I saw him, I want only to tell of a simple concern at the center of his life. He revealed it variously, and at different places. I remember one evening, walking with him from First Avenue toward midtown for our supper, that he was saying again, with increased earnestness, that "a good writer must be a good man." We had been talking about our contemporaries, and I had been saying that I believed that Faulkner—witness *As I Lay Dying*—was a writer with true tragic vision, albeit tormented. Tom agreed and insisted you can't be a good writer unless you are a good man; no matter how you suffer or which strange things you do, at bottom you can't be a good writer unless you are a good man. And as we crossed the street under the Third Avenue El, in the dim lights and strong noise of evening, he said, with real insistence, that Pope and Swift, no matter who said what, must have been good men, for they were good writers.

And in different context, on other occasions, he talked with me about what might be called "the break" with Maxwell Perkins and Scribner's. The thing was not what anguish had driven him to it, or any gains or losses there might be in it; the thing was this: having done what he had to do, was he still a good man?

I honor him for this conviction and for his effort to live by it. So many of us in our time have lost hold of this central concept that the first thing required of each of us—no matter what—is to be a good man. I believe the full measure and human greatness of Thomas Wolfe's life may be set down to the profound and un-relinquished hold he had on that concept, that by all power and all humility there was in him, by all effort and by all acceptance of grace, it was the ultimate purpose of his life to be a good man. For myself, somewhat cognizant of the wonders and terrors of human life, I never knew a better man. I never knew a man more courageous or more able at trying to fulfill the strange, haunting, and incomprehensible gift of our tragic human life. He knew now that each man must stop the beginning of evil first in himself. He faced the full tragic challenge of our human life, and his living of his life was a high, honorable fulfillment of manhood.

I saw him last in May of 1938. *Summer Song*, a verse play of mine was being produced at the Barbizon Plaza Theatre in New York, and Tom came to a matinee. A number of my friends from Newtown had also come to see it, and after the performance we all gathered downstairs in a lounge room.

Tom was heavy, grey of face, and very tired. He had his brief-

case jammed full of manuscript, and was presently going somewhere out of the city to meet and work with Mr. Aswell, the editor
at Harpers with whom he was now associated. From what he had
written me and told me I knew that during the past two and a
half years he had written, written, written, piling up the vast material of the last two long novels, and he and Aswell were at work
wresting publishable books out of this great matrix of creation.

He needed rest. But for all his weariness, he was genial to my
friends and very gentle toward me. One of my friends who saw
Thomas Wolfe only that once, that one half hour, tells me he still
remembers Wolfe for his candor, his courtesy, and his highly developed human goodness.

Even his hair no longer had the young and dark vitality of the
earlier years; it was thinning on his forehead and seemed to me
not so black. While he sat in a big chair and talked with us, his
heavy and bulging briefcase rested on the floor and against the
side of the chair. He still would sit with his left leg on his right
knee, and his right hand grasping his left ankle; he angled off a
great space of chair and floor sitting that way, and filled it with
the life of his talking. Meantime his silent briefcase, heavy on the
floor, was packed with written words that would endure.

I speculate, of course—but it is possible—when I say his
briefcase at that moment contained material of his final novel,
You Can't Go Home Again. I read this novel once more one summer in the White Mountains, seventeen years after last seeing
Thomas Wolfe face to face, and to me *You Can't Go Home Again*
is his own requiem. In that book he avows and relinquishes the
things in this world that he had loved and sought, desired and
won—his home town, the shining city, the love of woman, his
deepest friendship, and fame—and he envisages and accepts the
coming of his death. And there was finality in his relinquishment
of all these things of desire and achievement save only one. At the

point of death he called back for his friend, Maxwell Perkins; and Perkins came to his side. I believe that that afternoon he already knew and had already written down on pages perhaps there in his briefcase that his death was near.

He had to leave to catch a train. I went with him out of the basement lounge. He went ahead of me up the stairs toward daylight. On the sidewalk we clasped hands, looked into each other's eyes, and said goodbye for now. And for the last time I saw Thomas Wolfe's great figure in the midst of the tremendous city. For the last time, I clasped his warm hand and saw Thomas Wolfe's head against the sky.

The Last Word

I had hoped to see him again before Marguerite and I drove out to New Mexico for the summer with the children. But this did not come to pass. Early in July, out at the ranch where we were staying in Glencoe, New Mexico, I received a postcard from him. He had mailed it to Newtown and it had been forwarded to me. This postcard is a colored picture of Wizard Island in Crater Lake National Park, and it is postmarked Fort Klamath, Oregon, June 21, 1938. On it he wrote the last words I ever received from him:

Dear Bob: I'm covering the entire West and all the National Parks with some newspaper men. This is great country—this post card doesn't give you an idea of the beauty and magnificence of this place. Good luck and best wishes—Tom Wolfe.[15]

I was pleased to think of him travelling in the western regions of our continent, where I then was myself; I remembered how once before he had been west and had sent me from Santa Fe a postcard message to let me know he was visiting my home town; and I looked forward to seeing him in September when we both

[15] Unpublished letter, June 21, 1938.

should be back east again. While I was driving west with Marguerite and the children, taking our time for picnics and overnight stops, Tom must have passed me, still eager at a new seeing of the wild and beautiful earth, on one of the great trains he so loved, as it stroked the shining rails across the wonderful spread of our earth. And as we drove back east, toward home, he must have passed me again on another great train, but now a dying man, confined, fevered, and compressed in a Pullman space too small for the large and splendid man he was.

So it was that on September 15, 1938, Marguerite and the children and I reached St. Albans, Vermont, and put up for the night in the same hotel where Tom and I had passed a September night five years earlier, in 1933. The next morning I was up sooner than my family, and walked out of the hotel, bought a newspaper, and crossed the street to have breakfast in a restaurant where Tom and I had eaten breakfast. It was a narrow room, with darkish walls. I drank a glass of orange juice and began sipping my coffee before I looked at the newspaper.

Then I opened it and saw that my friend, Thomas Wolfe, had died only yesterday in a hospital in Baltimore.

That day I drove us south on the same route that Tom and I had followed south five years before, and I talked about him to Marguerite and the children more than I had ever before in my life talked about one man in one day. I stopped in Smuggler's Notch, where he and I had stopped, and showed the children great broken rocks which he and I had clambered, and showed them caves he and I had stooped into. All the way down the state of Vermont I showed them sights we had seen, places we had stopped, firm red brick houses in "Perkins' country" which Tom had admired.

I have never clearly thought of him as dead in a hospital in Baltimore; I see him in meteoric flash, like a terrible arc of fire, from Oregon to Maryland, his great life dying in his great frame, and his great brain dying by day and by night, in a train powerfully thundering across the vast and beautiful earth of America.

"Tiger! Tiger! burning bright..."

All that happened in my total association with Thomas Wolfe surpassed my understanding. On the first page I said that my friend was a religious poet; and now at the end I must say that each man's whole life is a religious experience, of a mystery and a wonder that exceeds even a tragic poet's song about it. Who, except by faith in the religious experience of conscious being, can account for the mystery of being alive at all? By the practical accounting of medicine, as understood by the doctor in attendance at the time, I was not expected to survive even the first morning of my birth. I cannot, except by religious wonder, account for the healthy birth of a child in North Carolina in 1900 and the perilous birth of another child in New Mexico in 1902, for their survival, their growth, their meetings, their years of friendship, and the death of the one before the other. It is by a religious apprehension that I have felt the fullness of these things, remembered them, and told them.

When we first met there was a profound difference between us in our view of life; it was, I believe, established for each of us in our infancy, and may have led to his intuitive gentleness toward me and my intuitive compassion toward him, which was perhaps the deepest binding of our friendship. For he was a well-borne child of beauty and vigor and health, his infancy shaped in instant and abounding life, which must have provoked responses of delight in the children and adults about his cradle, so that he probably never doubted, not for many, many years, his right to radiant and conquering life. I was a seven-months' child, and my fragile birth was followed by nine months of hovering in death, with periods of coma, with anxious adult faces watching over me, expecting death. Whereas I believe Tom enjoyed the normal man's primary strength in his profound feeling of the right to life, I know my spiritual strength from infancy has been that other one, of holding life, like a miracle, as purely a gift of God. But this difference between us, in our view of life, very deep when we first met, had almost vanished when we last parted, for by then he, too, had fully dwelt in the hovering of death. In the last letter he ever wrote—to Maxwell Perkins—he said:

I've made a long voyage and been to a strange country, and I've seen the dark man very close . . . and I know now I'm just a grain of dust, and I feel as if a great window has been opened on life I did not know about before—and if I come through this, I hope to God I am a better man, and in some strange way I can't explain, I know I am a deeper and a wiser one.[16]

I grieved when he died. He and I were both mountain-born and we both knew what it was to have the large and massive presence of mountains around the places of life. He would have understood the symbol of my grief for months following his death. I felt like a mountain man, who, with a sudden shock, finds himself on a broad plain with a flat horizon. His death was the falling away from my eyesight of a main mountain of my life.

Now already four times as many years have passed in knowing my friend is dead as the number of years I enjoyed in knowing him alive. How strange that he should die in young manhood, and that I should be the one to live beyond sixty years to tell it, even writing many of these pages with some of eleven grandchildren in the house where once he laughed with my children in their childhood. But one of the great gifts he gave me is still alive within me, and I have tried to share it in these pages. Thomas

---

[16] *Letters of Thomas Wolfe*, p. 777.

Wolfe gave me the direct mortal experience, and the still-living spiritual apprehension, of high manhood and deep friendship.

These are miracles in human life that surpass my understanding; I am thankful that they have touched my heart.

I abide with the sorrow of the death of my companion.

Newtown, Connecticut
November, 1942–May, 1965

BY ROBERT RAYNOLDS

BIOGRAPHICAL
Thomas Wolfe

ESSAYS
The Choice To Love
In Praise of Gratitude

NOVELS
Brothers in the West
Saunders Oak
Fortune
May Bretton
The Obscure Enemy
Paquita
The Sinner of Saint Ambrose
The Quality of Quiros
Far Flight of Love

DRAMA
Broadicea (verse)
The Ugly Runts (verse, produced, not published)
Summer Song (verse, produced, not published)
Farewell, Villon (produced, not published)

LIMITED EDITIONS
The Song of the Companion of God
Series of lectures, delivered at the Forty-Seventh Annual
Convocation of Congregational Ministers of Vermont. 250 copies.
Story Song
A book of stories and lyric poems. 50 copies.